Mathematical Dynamic Programming

First Edition

Aditya Chatterjee 🖐 Ue Kiao 🖐 Geoffrey Ziskovin

 OPENGENUS

© OpenGenus

BE A NATIONAL PROGRAMMER

INTRODUCTION

This book will change your Algorithmic Problem-Solving skills forever. Read it now to level up your future.

This book **"Mathematical Dynamic Programming"** is the only book you need to master Dynamic Programming. The focus is towards core Mathematical problems for Coding Interviews.

Many fail to solve basic DP problems such as Longest Increasing Subsequence and Shortest Common SuperSequence. All such problems are covered in this book in depth.

This book has covered 24 most important DP problems with detailed explanation along with sample implementations.

You should go through the implementations irrespective of the Programming Language you use as the ideas remain the same. Improving Implementation skills is important for Coding Interviews and this book will help you achieve it.

If you have time, you should read one chapter every day and think about the problem on your own. Try to find different variants.

These carefully selected problems will help you level up your skills and help secure a good job or internship soon.

Get started with this book and change the equation of your career.

Book: **Mathematical Dynamic Programming**

Authors (3): Aditya Chatterjee, Ue Kiao, Geoffrey Ziskovin

About the authors:

Aditya Chatterjee is an Independent Researcher, Technical Author and the Founding Member of OPENGENUS, a scientific community focused on Computing Technology.

Ue Kiao is a Japanese Software Developer and has played key role in designing systems like TaoBao, AliPay and many more. She has completed her B. Sc in Mathematics and Computing Science at National Taiwan University and PhD at Tokyo Institute of Technology.

Geoffrey Ziskovin is an American Software Engineer with an experience of over 30 years. He has interviewed over 700 candidates worldwide for various Fortune 500 companies.

Published: May 2022 (Edition 1)

Publisher: © OpenGenus

ISBN: 9798831194098

Contact: team@opengenus.org

Available on Amazon as Paperback.

© **OpenGenus**

Table of Contents

Recommended Books

- <u>Linked List Problems</u>: For Interviews and Competitive Programming
- <u>Problems on Array</u>
- <u>Binary Tree Problems</u>
- <u>Dynamic Programming on Trees</u>

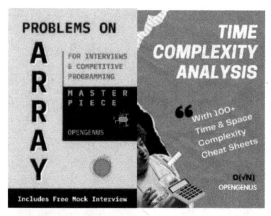

- <u>Day before Coding Interview</u> series
- <u>#7daysOfAlgo</u> series

Introduction to Dynamic Programming

Dynamic Programming is the technique of utilizing the answer of smaller problem set to find the answer of a larger problem set.

DP(N1) = F(DP(M1), DP(M2), ..., DP(MP))

where:

- DP(j) is the answer for a problem set of size j

- DP denotes Dynamic Programming as a convention

- Mi and N1 are problem sizes

- M1, M2, ..., MP < N1

- F is the function of how smaller values DP(Mi) are used

This is the mathematical formulation of Dynamic Programming.

Note a larger problem set that is DP(N1) is using the values of smaller problem sets to calculate the answer. The value of a smaller problem set in-turn depend on smaller problem sets and are pre-computed.

An easily example is the formulation of factorial F(N) where:

F(N) = N! = 1 * 2 * 3 * ... * (N-1) * N

F(N-1) = (N-1)! = 1 * 2 * 3 * ... * (N-2) * (N-1)

F(N) = F(N-1) * N

In this case, calculating F(N) that is N! by the basic formulation requires N-1 multiplication but if we have the answer to F(N-1) that is (N-1)!, then we can find the answer to F(N) that is N! with just 1 multiplication.

This improves the complexity from O(N) to O(1) for this data point.

If you observe carefully, with N-1 multiplications, we can find all values of F(i) for i >= 1 and i <= N. This results in O(N) time complexity.

This is an improvement as with the basic approach finding values of all N values will take O(N2) time.

The above problem works on one data point. These problems are usually identified as having a formula to directly compute a specific data point.

The use of Dynamic Programming in this case is to generate all such data points sequentially with a better performance. Consider the case of using Dynamic

Programming to compute all factorials for 1 to N and you will get the idea.

For some problems, the advantage of Dynamic Programming lies in finding one specific data point (instead of a range or sequence of data points). The idea will be clear as we move to solve Practice Problems.

Dynamic Programming on Mathematical Problems

Categories of Mathematical Problems where Dynamic Programming is applicable are:

- Problems involving combinatorics and permutation
- Finding a sub-sequence with a property
- Generating a sequence
- Finding subsets with a property

Problems involving combinatorics and permutation

Permutation and Combination is the core of Mathematical problems where we need to find the total number of possibilities.

Permutation $P(n, k)$ is defined as the number of combinations of getting K elements in order from a set of N elements. It equates to the following:

$$P(n,k) = n.(n-1).(n-2)...(n-k+1) = n!/(n-k)!$$

As Dynamic Programming requires, Permutation depends on smaller values of permutation:

4

P(n,k) = P(n-1, k) + k * P(n-1, k-1)

Similarly, Combination C(n, k) is defined as the number of combinations of getting K elements (no order) from a set of N elements. It equates to the following:

C(n,k) = n! / [k! (n-k)!]

As Combination is a special case of Permutation, it follows the DP structure.

C(n, k) * k! = P(n, k)

In practice problems, you will understand how Dynamic Programming exploits this basic feature to solve several Mathematical Problems efficiently.

One key technique is to reduce a problem or link it to an existing problem where a Dynamic Programming solution exists.

Finding a sub-sequence with a property

Examples of problems where we need to find a sub-sequence with a property are:

5

- Longest Increasing Subsequence
- Longest Decreasing Subsequence
- Longest Common Increasing Subsequence

In a set of N elements, there are 2^N subsequences. This is an exponential size so brute force is not a feasible solution.

The only way to identify a specific subsequence with a given property is to:

- Identify sub-problems that follow DP structure
- Apply DP to find the subsequence in polynomial time

The key is to think if you have the answer of the first N-1 elements, then how can you use the answer to find the answer of the complete set of N elements.

Generating a sequence

Examples of problems where we need to generate a sequence are:

- Newman Conway Sequence
- n^{th} Fibonacci number

These are case where:

- the Nth element in a sequence is derived using previous elements of the sequence
- there is no direct formula to compute N^{th} element OR a direct formula is computationally expensive

In such cases, Dynamic Programming can find a relatively efficient approach to generate multiple elements of the sequence at once.

Finding subsets with a property

Example of problems where we need to find subsets with a property are:

- Find if a Subset with sum divisible by m exist

This is similar to the category "Finding a sub-sequence with a property".

If you look carefully, these are a kind of optimization problems. These are several possibilities (generally, exponential) and we need to traverse through all possibilities to find the one which is our answer.

Dynamic Programming starts with smaller values and:

7

- Either traverse significantly less possibilities
- Checks only combinations that follow one another and eventually, reaches the answer
- Traverses through possibilities in a structured way

On going through multiple examples in this book, you will understand how Dynamic Programming is applied in Mathematical Problems.

Longest Increasing Subsequence

In this problem, we have a set of data and we have to find the longest subsequence which is in increasing order.

Example:

Given set: 1, 9, 19, 17, 32, 15, 99

Longest Increasing Subsequence: 1, 9, 17, 32, 99

Other increasing subsequences are:

- 1, 19, 32, 99
- 1, 19, 15, 99
- 1, 9, 15, 99
- 1, 9, 99

and many more such subsequences.

The brute force approach to solve this is to generate all subsequences, check if the current subsequence is in increasing order and keep track of the longest such subsequence.

The time complexity of this brute force approach is $O(2^N xN)$ as:

- There are $O(2^N)$ subsequences for N elements
- It takes $O(N)$ time to check if a subsequence is in increasing order

The space complexity is $O(1)$ as we need not store the current subsequence and it can be represented as a bit sequence.

As this takes exponential time, we must improve it and we can use a Dynamic Programming based approach.

9

The structure is as follows:

```
dp[i] = Length of Longest Increasing
        Subsequence where the last element
        is the i^th element A[i]
```

The base case is:

```
dp[i] = 1 (by default)
```

This is because a single element satisfies both conditions.

The recursive relation is:

```
dp[i] = 1 + maximum(dp[j])
        where 0 < j < i AND a[j] <= a[i]
```

The answer is the maximum value in the DP array.

We calculate the values in bottom-up approach. Following is the pseudocode of our Dynamic Programming approach:

```
dp[0] = 1;

for (int i = 1; i < n; i++)
{
    dp[i] = 1;
    for (int j = 0; j < i; j++ )
        if (a[i] > a[j] AND dp[i] < dp[j] + 1)
            dp[i] = dp[j] + 1;
}
```

The time complexity of this approach is $O(N^2)$ as for the calculation of each value, we go through all previous values.

The space complexity is $O(N)$.

The summary of our time and space complexity is as follows:

Approach	Time Complexity	Space Complexity
Brute Force	$O(2^N \times N)$	$O(1)$
Dynamic Programming	$O(N^2)$	$O(N)$

With this, we achieve an exponential improvement.

© **OpenGenus**

Longest Decreasing Subsequence

In this problem, we have a set of data and we have to find the longest subsequence which is in decreasing order.

The approach is similar to our previous problem "**Longest Increasing Subsequence**".

Example:

Given set: 10, -1, 4, 7, 0, 5, 2, -1

Longest Decreasing Subsequence: 10, 7, 5, 2, -1

Other decreasing subsequences are:

- 10, -1
- 10, 4, 2, -1
- 7, -1
- 10, 7, 2, -1

and many more such subsequences.

The brute force approach to solve this is to generate all subsequences, check if the current subsequence is in decreasing order and keep track of the longest such subsequence.

The time complexity of this brute force approach is $O(2^N \times N)$ as:

- There are $O(2^N)$ subsequences for N elements
- It takes $O(N)$ time to check if a subsequence is in decreasing order

12

The space complexity is O(1) as we need not store the current subsequence and it can be represented as a bit sequence.

As this takes exponential time, we must improve it and we can use a Dynamic Programming based approach.

The structure is as follows:

```
dp[i] = Length of Longest Decreasing
        Subsequence where the last
        element is the ith element A[i]
```

The base case is:

```
dp[i] = 1 (by default)
```

This is because a single element satisfies both conditions.

The recursive relation is:

```
dp[i] = 1 + maximum(dp[j])
        where 0 < j < i AND a[j] >= a[i]
```

The answer is the maximum value in the DP array.

Note: the condition a[j] >= a[i] is the difference from the previous problem "Longest Increasing Subsequence".

We calculate the values in bottom-up approach. Following is the pseudocode of our Dynamic Programming approach:

```
dp[0] = 1;

for (int i = 1; i < n; i++)
{
    dp[i] = 1;
    for (int j = 0; j < i; j++ )
        if (a[i] < a[j] AND dp[i] < dp[j] + 1)
            dp[i] = dp[j] + 1;
}
```

The time complexity of this approach is $O(N^2)$ as for the calculation of each value, we go through all previous values.

The space complexity is $O(N)$.

The summary of our time and space complexity is as follows:

Approach	Time Complexity	Space Complexity
Brute Force	$O(2^N \times N)$	$O(1)$
Dynamic Programming	$O(N^2)$	$O(N)$

With this, we achieve an exponential improvement.

Longest Common Increasing Subsequence

In this problem, we have 2 set of elements and we need to find the longest common subsequence such that the subsequence is in increasing order.

Example:

Given arrays:

a1 = {2,6,4,9}

a2 = {3,4,2,7,9,6}

The answer would be {2, 9} as this is the longest common subsequence which is also increasing.

The brute force approach is to generate all subsequences in the first set S1 of N elements, check if the subsequence in present in the second set S2 of M elements and if the subsequence is in increasing order. We need to keep track of the length of the longest such subsequence.

This brute force approach takes $O(2^N \times (N+M))$ time as:

- There are $O(2^N)$ subsequences in a set of N elements
- It takes $O(M)$ time to check if the subsequence is present in a set of M elements
- It takes $O(N)$ time to check if the subsequence is in increasing order

In terms of space complexity, our brute force approach will take O(1) space as we need not store the subsequence and instead represent it using a bitmap.

We can improve the approach using a Dynamic Programming approach.

Let the two arrays be arr1 and arr2.

The Dynamic Programming structure is as follows:

```
dp[j] = length of Longest common increasing
        subsequence ending with arr2[j]
```

For filling values in this dp array, we traverse all elements of arr1[] and for every element in arr1[i], we traverse all elements of arr2[].

If we find a match, we update dp[j] with length of current LCIS. To maintain current LCIS, we keep checking valid dp[j] values.

The relation is as follows:

```
# if a common element is found in both arrays
if arr1[i] == arr2[j]:
    dp[j] = max(current+1, dp[j])
```

```
# if arr1 element is greater, current variable
is updated
if arr1[i] > arr2[j]:
    current = max(current, dp[j])
```

Pseudocode

- Creating a dp table of length same as arr2 and elements as 0.
- Start traversing all elements of arr2 for each element of arr1.
- If a common element is found, current variable is incremented and is stored in dp array.
- If element of arr1 is greater than element of arr2, we update our current variable with the maximum of current or the value stored in dp at that index.
- After all elements of arr1 is covered, we return the maximum value from our dp table as result.

The pseudocode is as follows:

```
l1 = length(arr1)
l2 = length(arr2)

# Creating our dp table that will store the
length of LCIS ending at arr2[j]
dp[l2]

# Traversing all elements of arr1
```

```
for i from 0 to 11:

    # Variable to store length of current LCIS
    current = 0

    # Traversing all elements of arr2
    for j in range(12):

        # if a common element is found in both
arrays
        if arr1[i] == arr2[j]:
            dp[j] = max(current+1, dp[j])

        # if arr1 element is greater,
        # current variable is updated
        if arr1[i] > arr2[j]:
            current = max(current, dp[j])

# final result for LCIS
answer = maximum(dp)
```

Example:

Suppose we have arr1 as [2,4,9,1] and arr2 as [2,5,8,4,9,0,1].

Length of both arrays are taken in l1 and l2 variables as l1 = 4 and l2 = 7.

An array with elements as 0 and length same as l2 is declared. Our dp array will look like: [0,0,0,0,0,0,0]

We start traversing all elements of arr2 for each element of arr1.

When we find a common element, we update our dp table at that index and if we find arr1 element greater than arr2 element, we update out current variable accordingly.

After traversing first element of arr1, and all elements of arr2, our dp table will look like: [1,0,0,0,0,0,0] as first element of both arrays were common and current variable at that time was 0.

Similarly, for all elements of arr1, exact process is repeated, our dp table at end would like: [1,0,0,2,3,0,1].

At end, maximum value from this dp table is our answer which is LCIS=3.

The time complexity of our Dynamic Programming approach will be **O(NxM)** with space complexity of O(M).

The summary of the approach is as follows:

Approach	Time Complexity	Space Complexity
Brute Force	$O(2^N x(N+M))$	$O(1)$
Dynamic Programming	$O(NxM)$	$O(M)$

Longest Common Decreasing Subsequence

In this problem, we have 2 set of elements and we need to find the longest common subsequence such that the subsequence is in decreasing order.

This is similar to our previous problem "Longest Common Increasing Subsequence".

Example:

Given arrays:

a1 = {9, 4, 6, 2}

a2 = {6, 9, 7, 2, 4, 3}

The answer would be {9, 2} as this is the longest common subsequence which is also decreasing. There are other subsequences of length 2 that satisfies the conditions.

The brute force approach is to generate all subsequences in the first set S1 of N elements, check if the subsequence in present in the second set S2 of M elements and if the subsequence is in decreasing order. We need to keep track of the length of the longest such subsequence.

This brute force approach takes $O(2^N \times (N+M))$ time as:

- There are $O(2^N)$ subsequences in a set of N elements

- It takes O(M) time to check if the subsequence is present in a set of M elements
- It takes O(N) time to check if the subsequence is in decreasing order

In terms of space complexity, our brute force approach will take O(1) space as we need not store the subsequence and instead represent it using a bitmap.

We can improve the approach using a Dynamic Programming approach.

Let the two arrays be arr1 and arr2.

The Dynamic Programming structure is as follows:

```
dp[j] = length of Longest common decreasing
        subsequence ending with arr2[j]
```

For filling values in this dp array, we traverse all elements of arr1[] and for every element in arr1[i], we traverse all elements of arr2[].

If we find a match, we update dp[j] with length of current LCDS. To maintain current LCDS, we keep checking valid dp[j] values.

The relation is as follows:

```
# if a common element is found in both arrays
if arr1[i] == arr2[j]:
    dp[j] = max(current+1, dp[j])


# if arr1 element is greater, current variable
is updated
if arr1[i] < arr2[j]:
    current = max(current, dp[j])
```

Pseudocode

- Creating a dp table of length same as arr2 and elements as 0.
- Start traversing all elements of arr2 for each element of arr1.
- If a common element is found, current variable is incremented and is stored in dp array.
- If element of arr1 is smaller than element of arr2, we update our current variable with the maximum of current or the value stored in dp at that index.
- After all elements of arr1 is covered, we return the maximum value from our dp table as result.

The pseudocode is as follows:

```
l1 = length(arr1)
l2 = length(arr2)

# Creating our dp table that will store the
length of LCDS ending at arr2[j]
dp[l2]

# Traversing all elements of arr1
for i from 0 to l1:

    # Variable to store length of current LCDS
    current = 0

    # Traversing all elements of arr2
    for j in range(l2):

        # if a common element is found in both
arrays
        if arr1[i] == arr2[j]:
            dp[j] = max(current+1, dp[j])

        # if arr1 element is greater,
        # current variable is updated
        if arr1[i] < arr2[j]:
            current = max(current, dp[j])

# Final result for LCDS
answer = maximum(dp)
```

Example:

Suppose we have arr1 as [1, 9, 4, 2] and arr2 as [1, 0, 9, 4, 8 , 5, 2].

Length of both arrays are taken in l1 and l2 variables as l1 = 4 and l2 = 7.

An array with elements as 0 and length same as l2 is declared. Our dp array will look like: [0,0,0,0,0,0,0]

We start traversing all elements of arr2 for each element of arr1.

When we find a common element, we update our dp table at that index and if we find arr1 element greater than arr2 element, we update out current variable accordingly.

After traversing first element of arr1, and all elements of arr2, our dp table will look like: [1,0,0,0,0,0,0] as first element of both arrays were common and current variable at that time was 1.

Similarly, for all elements of arr1, exact process is repeated, our dp table at end would like: [1,2,2,2,2,2,2].

At end, maximum value from this dp table is our answer which is LCDS=2.

The time complexity of our Dynamic Programming approach will be **O(NxM)** with space complexity of O(M).

The summary of the approach is as follows:

Approach	Time Complexity	Space Complexity
Brute Force	$O(2^N x(N+M))$	$O(1)$
Dynamic Programming	$O(NxM)$	$O(M)$

Note: The approach is same as the previous approach. This is because increasing and decreasing are same class of relative operation. If we consider another class of operation like addition, the approach will change. Think about this.

Longest Increasing Odd Even Subsequence

In this problem, we are an array of N elements and we need to find the longest subsequence such that every alternative element is odd and even starting with odd number and all elements in the subsequence is in increasing order.

Example:

Given array:

arr = {5,6,2,1,7,4,8,3}

Our output will be 4, as {5,6,7,8} is the longest subsequence having alternate odd and even elements.

The brute force approach will be to generate all subsequences, check if the subsequence has odd and even elements consecutively and is in increasing order and keep a track of the length of the longest subsequence that satisfies the condition.

This brute force approach takes $O(2^N \times N)$ time as:

- There are $O(2^N)$ subsequences
- It takes $O(N)$ time to verify if a subsequence is satisfying the condition

So, our Efficient approach would be to use Dynamic programming to solve this problem.

We store the longest increasing odd-even sub-sequence ending at each index of given arr[]. We create an auxiliary array dp[] such that dp[j] stores length of Longest increasing odd even subsequence or LIOES ending with arr[j]. At the end, we return maximum value from this array.

```
dp[j] = length of Longest increasing odd
        even subsequence ending with arr[j]
```

For filling values in this dp array, we traverse all elements of arr[] and for each element, we traverse all elements of same array till that position and check for our conditions.

If it satisfies all the conditions, we update dp[j] with length of current LIOES.

```
if (arr[i] > arr[j]
    and (arr[i]+arr[j]) % 2 != 0
    and dp[i] < dp[j] + 1)
        dp[i] = dp[j] + 1
```

Pseudocode

- Create a dp table of length same as given array and elements as 1, because each element of given array is a subsequence itself.
- Start traversing all elements of arr and for each element, traverse all the elements till that position again checking for conditions.
- If all the conditions are satisfied, that position in dp[] array is incremented.
- Conditions we check for are: arr[i]>arr[j] and (arr[i] + arr[j]) % 2 != 0 and dp[i] < dp[j] + 1 where, i is iterator of primary loop and j is iterator of secondary loop.
- After our primary loop is completed, we return the maximum value of our dp array.

```
# Taking length of given array
l = len(arr)

# Creating the DP table of length l and
elements as 1
dp[] = [1]*l

# Primary loop
for i in range(1,n):

    # Secondary loop
    for j in range(i):

        # Checking for conditions
        if (arr[i] > arr[j] and (arr[i]+arr[j])
% 2 != 0 and dp[i] < dp[j] + 1):
```

```
              # Incrementing value in dp table
              dp[i] = dp[j] + 1

# maximum value from DP array
ANSWER = maximum(dp)
```

Workflow of solution

Suppose we have our input array arr1 as [2,7,3,4,9,1].

Length of array is taken in l variable as l = 6.

An array with elements as 1 and length same as l is declared.
Our dp array will look like: [1,1,1,1,1,1]

We start traversing all elements of arr and for each element, we
traverse same array again till that position.

When we find an element in secondary loop, that is smaller
than our current element of primary loop and satisfies the odd-
even condition and length of LIOES at that position + 1 is greater
that LIOES of current primary loop position than we increment
our dp table at that index.

After traversing on second element of arr, and all elements of
same arr till second element, our dp table will look like:
[1,2,1,1,1,1] as first element of arr satisfies all the conditions

mentioned above, we incremented the our dp table at second position.

Similarly, for third elements of arr, exact process is repeated, and as first element again satisfies all conditions our dp table would look like: [1,2,2,1,1,1]. Here we incremented our third element of dp array.

After our primary loop is completed, our dp table would look like: [1,2,2,3,4,1]

At end, maximum value from this dp table is returned by function as our LIOES=4.

Complexity of our Dynamic Programming approach

As we traverse all elements of arr twice in a nested loop, our time complexity would be $O(N^2)$, where n is length of array.

For storing all LIOES for each element of arr, we created an array of size N, so our space complexity would be $O(N)$.

The summary of time and space complexity is as follows:

Approach	Time Complexity	Space Complexity
Brute Force	$O(2^N x(N))$	$O(1)$
Dynamic Programming	$O(N^2)$	$O(N)$

This is an important problem as we have considered multiple conditions for our subsequences. Notice how it changed the solution structure and recursive relations. Think over it.

Shortest Common SuperSequence

Given two strings X and Y, the supersequence of string X and Y is such a string Z that both X and Y is subsequence of Z. In other words, shortest supersequence of X and Y is smallest possible string Z such that all the alphabets of both the strings occurs in Z and in same order as of the original string.

In this problem, we have two input strings S1 and S2 and we need to find the shortest common supersequence.

Example:

- X = "opengenus"
- Y = "operagenes"

shortest common supersequence of X and Y:

Z = "openragenues"

and length of z is 12

We can see that both "opengenus" and "operagenes" is subsequence of "openragenues".

There can be more than one shortest common supersequence, in that case we may consider any of them as the length of the supersequence will be the same.

Here we will see two approaches to find the minimum length of common supersequence and how to print a shortest common suersequence.

Brute force approach

The brute force approach can be more challenging for this problem. The idea is the resultant string can be a maximum length of 2N for two input strings of length N.

The minimum length will be N. So, in terms of length, there will be N groups of strings.

For each group of length J (where J >= N and J <= 2N), we need to generate all permutations. There will be J! permutations.

For each group of length J, we get J number of groups of length J-1. So, the permutations of all groups of length J will be (J-1)! x J = J!.

Hence, we arrive at the fact that there will be N x (2N)! potential strings. For each string, we need to verify that both input strings are substrings which can be verified in linear time O(N).

Hence, the time complexity of this brute force approach will be O(N x N x (2N)!) = O(N^{N+2}) = **O(N^N)** which is exponential.

Dynamic Programming approach

From the brute force approach, we know that the size of our search space is O(N^N). We need to efficiently find the answer by utilizing the structure of the search space using Dynamic Programming.

```
dp[i][j] = length of shortest common
           supersequence of First i characters
           of string S1 and First j characters
           of string S2
```

The base case is that if one string is empty (length = 0), then the length of the answer is same as that of the length of the other string (second string is the answer).

```
dp[i][j] = j        if i == 0
dp[i][j] = i        if j == 0
```

If the ith character of string S1 and j^{th} character of string S2, then the answer of dp[i][j] will be 1 + length of shortest common supersequence with first (i-1) characters of S1 and first (j-1) characters of S2.

```
dp[i][j] = dp[i - 1][j - 1] + 1
```

```
if S1[i] == S2[j]
```

If the above condition does not satisfy, then two cases may take place:

In this case, as i^{th} character of S1 is not same as j^{th} character of S2. Hence, either i^{th} character of S1 or j^{th} character of S2 or both is included in the final answer.

- i^{th} character of string S1 is included in answer

In this case, the answer of length of shortest common supersequence for first i^{th} character of string S1 and first j^{th} character of string S2 is 1 (for including the ith string) + length of shortest common supersequence for first $(i-1)^{th}$ character of string S1 and first j^{th} character of string S2.

- j^{th} character of string S2 is included in answer

In this case, the answer of length of shortest common supersequence for first i^{th} character of string S1 and first j^{th} character of string S2 is 1 (for including the jth string) + length of shortest common supersequence for first i^{th} character of string S1 and first $(j-1)^{th}$ character of string S2.

As we need to find the shortest such string, the minimum of the above two value is our answer.

```
dp[i][j] = 1 + MINIMUM(dp[i - 1][j],
```

```
                      dp[i][j - 1])
```

The complete pseudocode is as follows:

```
// 1 extra index as dp[0][0] denotes empty
input
dp[length(str1) + 1][length(str1) + 1]

for i from 0 to (length(str1)+1):
    for j from 0 to (length(str2)+1):
        if i == 0:
            dp[i][j] = j
        else if j == 0:
            dp[i][j] = i
        else if str1[i - 1] == str2[j - 1]:
            dp[i][j] = dp[i - 1][j - 1] + 1
        else:
            dp[i][j] =1 + min(dp[i - 1][j],
dp[i][j - 1])

  answer = dp[length(str1)][length(str2)]
```

The time complexity of this approach is O(length of first string X length of second string) = $O(N^2)$.

To imagine the wonder of this, read and understand the following statement carefully:

In the search space, there are $O(N^N)$ elements and one element is our answer. To find the answer, we just checked $O(N^2)$ elements that is we know only one thing of the rest $O(N^{N-2})$ elements that is none of the elements in the set is the answer.

Following table summarizes the performance improvement:

Approach	Time Complexity	Space Complexity
Brute Force	$O(N^N)$	$O(1)$
Dynamic Programming	$O(N^2)$	$O(N^2)$

This is an important problem as we have explored the reverse strategy in terms of our previous problems but still managed to gain similar performance.

© **OpenGenus**

Maximum Sum Subsequence

This may seem to be a simple problem but is important to understand the following few problems which we will work on. We will see how incremental changes in the problem statement changes the solution.

This problem "**Maximum Sum Subsequence**" is to find the length of the subsequence with the maximum sum.

For example:

Input: 2 -1 0 4 5 -10 -4 9

Answer: Sequence {2, 0, 4, 5, 9} has the maximum sum 20 with length 5.

Note that the sequence {2, 4, 5, 9} also has sum 20 but with length 4.

Brute force approach

For a set of N elements, there will be 2^N subsequences and to check the sum of a given subsequence, the time required is O(N). This brings the time complexity to O(N x 2^N).

The space complexity will be O(1) as we do not need to store any subsequence using the previous techniques we demonstrated.

The steps are:

- Generate all subsequences
- For each subsequence:
    - Check if it has the maximum sum
- Maximum sum is our answer

Note: We have covered the idea of generating all subsequences in previous problems (Hint: Use bit notation of integers)

Greedy Approach

If you observe carefully, you will understand that to get the maximum sum, we just need to consider positive numbers as negative numbers will always reduce the sum.

If there is no positive number, then our answer is 0 corresponding to an empty set.

Hence, the steps are:

- Traverse through all elements of the set one by one
    - If current element is >= 0, then include it in the answer (answer = answer + current element)

This is a simple algorithm and requires only one traversal.

The pseudocode is as follows:

```
array A of N elements
N = length(A)
int dp[N]
sum = 0

for i from 1 to length(A)
```

```
      if A[i] >= 0
          sum += A[i]

answer = sum
```

Hence, this approach using Greedy Algorithm takes:

- O(N) time complexity
- O(1) space complexity

Dynamic Programming Approach

With the Greedy algorithm we have achieved optimal performance (as we must check all elements at least once) but this problem can be formulated as a Dynamic Programming problem with same performance.

Our basic structure dp[i] is as follows:

```
dp[i] = Sum of maximum sum subset with i^th
        element as the last element of the
        subset
```

Due to the structure of the problem and the property we saw in our greedy algorithm approach, we know the answer for N elements can be generated on just checking the Nth element if we have the answer for the first N-1 elements.

© **OpenGenus**

This recursive relation is captured by the following relation:

```
dp[i] = 1 + dp[i - 1]     ......  if dp[i] >= 0
      = dp[i - 1]         ......  if dp[i] < 0
```

The answer for N elements will be the last element that is dp[N-1].

The pseudocode is as follows:

```
array A of N elements
N = length(A)
int dp[N]

if A[0] >= 0
    dp[0] = A[0]
else
    dp[0] = 0

for i from 1 to length(A)
    if A[i] >= 0
        dp[i] = dp[i-1] + 1

answer = dp[N-1]
```

The performance/ complexity of our Dynamic Programming approach is as follows:

- Time complexity: O(N)
- Space complexity: O(N)

This is summarized by the following table:

Approach	Time Complexity	Space Complexity
Brute Force	$O(N \times 2^N)$	$O(1)$
Greedy Algorithm	$O(N)$	$O(1)$
Dynamic Programming	$O(N)$	$O(N)$

For this case, the greedy algorithm may seem to be better as it takes constant additional space, but the Dynamic Programming solution is significant as we extend the problem.

Maximum Sum Subsequence of size K

In this problem, we are given a set of N elements and we need to find the sum of the subsequence which:

- Has the maximum sum
- Has exactly K elements

For example:

Input: {19, -1, 2, 8, 10, -2, 20} and K = 3

In this, the subsequence satisfying our conditions of maximum sum and increasing order is:

{2, 8, 10} with sum = 20

{2, 8, 20} with sum = 30

{2, 10, 20} with sum = 32

{19, 10, 20} with sum = 49

And so on ...

The maximum sum subsequence satisfying the conditions is {19, 10, 20} with sum 49.

Note that in this problem, one fact changes that negative numbers can become a part of the answer.

Consider the case:

Input elements: {-1, -9, 5, 10} and K = 3

In this case, our answer will be {-1, 5, 10} with sum 14. We had to consider a negative number -1 as we had to take 3 elements for our answer.

Brute force approach

The brute force approach will be similar to the previous problem with one extra condition that is the size is pre-defined.

The brute force approach is to generate all subsequences and for each subsequence, we need to check if there are K elements and keep track of the largest sum.

For N elements, there will be $O(2^N)$ subsequences and to check the conditions, it would take $O(N)$ time for each subsequence.

With this, the time complexity will be $O(N \times 2^N)$ with constant space complexity $O(1)$.

The steps are:

- Generate all subsequences
- For each subsequence:
  - Check if it has the maximum sum and consists of K elements
- Maximum sum is our answer

Note: We have covered the idea of generating all subsequences in previous problems (Hint: Use bit notation of integers)

Note: There is no viable Greedy Algorithm solution to this problem like the previous problem.

Dynamic Programming approach

The structure of our Dynamic Programming approach is as follows:

```
dp[i][j] = Sum of Largest sum subset with first
           i elements and length j with the jth
           element as the last element in the
           subsequence
```

The base case are as follows:

- If j (length of subsequence) is 0, then the answer is 0 as no element can be included.
- If i (considering first i elements) is 0, then the answer is 0 as no element is being considered for the answer.
- If j (length of subsequence) is 1, then the answer will be the ith element as one element needs to be included and i^{th} element should be the last element (based on our structure).

```
dp[i][0] = 0      ......    for all i from 0 to N
dp[0][j] = 0      ......    for all j from 0 to N
dp[i][1] = A[i]   ......    for all i fron 0 to N
```

Think of the relation with which we can calculate the values.

The maximum sub sequence of size j with first i elements will be the maximum of all values that are of (size j-1 with any element among the first i-1 elements as the last element) + the ith element (as it should be the last element).

Understand this intuitively:

For size j with i^{th} element last element, if we remove the last element, we get:

A set of j-1 elements with the last element being one from the first i-1 elements. We need to find the maximum of this value in together with the addition of the ith element.

Note: You may think that the sum of ith element can be handled separately but this is not possible as the answer may include negative numbers.

Think about this point.

With this, our relation is as follows:

```
// Compute the relation
for i from 1 to N
    for j from 0 to i-1
        for m from 1 to K (size)
            dp[i][1 + 1] = MAXIMUM(dp[i][1 +
1],

                          dp[j][1] + A[i])
```

The complete pseudocode is as follows:

```
array A of N elements, K (size)
N = length(A)
int dp[N][N]

// Base case
for i from 0 to N
    dp[i][0] = 0
    dp[0][i] = 0
    dp[i][1] = A[i]

// Compute the relation
for i from 1 to N
    for j from 0 to i-1
        for m from 1 to K (size)
            dp[i][1 + 1] = MAXIMUM(dp[i][1 +
1],
                            dp[j][1] + A[i])

// Find the maximum value
answer = 0
for i from 0 to N
    if answer < dp[i][K]
        answer = dp[i][K]
```

With this, the complexity of our Dynamic Programming approach is as follows:

- Time complexity: $O(N^2)$
- Space complexity: $O(N^2)$

This is summarized by the following table:

Approach	Time Complexity	Space Complexity
Brute Force	$O(N \times 2^N)$	$O(1)$
Dynamic Programming	$O(N^2)$	$O(N^2)$

Note that how adding a condition that the subsequence should be of size K changed the following:

- Time complexity: Increased from $O(N)$ to $O(N^2)$
- Space complexity: Increased from $O(N)$ to $O(N^2)$

Maximum Sum Increasing Subsequence

In this problem, we are given N elements and we need to find the sum of the elements in the largest subsequence with maximum sum and increasing order.

For example:

Input: {9, -1, 2, 8, 10, -2, 20}

In this, the subsequence satisfying our conditions of maximum sum and increasing order is:

{2, 8, 10, 20} with sum = 40

Brute force approach

The brute force approach is to generate all subsequences and for each subsequence, we need to check if the elements are in increasing order and keep track of the largest sum.

For N elements, there will be $O(2^N)$ subsequences and to check the conditions, it would take $O(N)$ time for each subsequence.

With this, the time complexity will be $O(N \times 2^N)$ with constant space complexity $O(1)$.

The steps are:

- Generate all subsequences
- For each subsequence:
    - Check if it has the maximum sum and if it is in increasing order

- Maximum sum is our answer

Note: We have covered the idea of generating all subsequences in previous problems (Hint: Use bit notation of integers)

Note: There is no viable Greedy Algorithm solution to this problem. One thing we know for certain is that even in this problem, negative numbers will not be a part of the solution.

Dynamic Programming Approach

If you notice carefully, this problem is the merge of two problems that we have explored previously:

- Longest sum subsequence problem
- Longest Increasing Subsequence problem

The "Longest Sum Subsequence" problem takes $O(N)$ time complexity with $O(N)$ space complexity for N elements.

The "Longest Increasing Subsequence" problem takes $O(N^2)$ time complexity with $O(N)$ space complexity for N elements.

The structure of our Dynamic Programming solution is as follows:

```
dp[i] = Sum of Longest Increasing subset with
        ith element as the last element of the
        subset
```

The base case is that the answer with the last element fixed is the last element itself (in case, the other elements are not considered).

```
// Base case
for i from 0 to N
    dp[i] = A[i] // i-th element
```

The recursive relation is as follows:

```
// Compute the recursive relation
for i from 1 to N
    for j from 0 to i-1
        if A[i] > A[j]
            if dp[i] < dp[j] + A[i]
                dp[i] = dp[j] + A[i];
```

The pseudocode is as follows:

```
array A of N elements
N = length(A)
int dp[N]

// Base case
for i from 0 to N
    dp[i] = A[i] // i-th element

// Compute the recursive relation
for i from 1 to N
    for j from 0 to i-1
        if A[i] > A[j]
            if dp[i] < dp[j] + A[i]
```

```
                dp[i] = dp[j] + A[i];

// Find the maximum value
answer = 0
for i from 0 to N
    if answer < dp[i]
        answer = dp[i]
```

With this approach, we have achieved the following
complexities:

- $O(N^2)$ time complexity
- $O(N)$ space complexity

This is summarized by the following table:

Approach	Time Complexity	Space Complexity
Brute Force	$O(N \times 2^N)$	$O(1)$
Dynamic Programming	$O(N^2)$	$O(N)$

Note that how adding a condition that the subsequence should
be in increasing order changed the following:

- Time complexity: $O(N)$ to $O(N^2)$
- Space complexity remained same: $O(N)$

We will add a further condition to this problem in our next
problem and see how it impacts the solution.

© **OpenGenus**

Maximum Sum Increasing Subsequence of size K

In this problem, we are given a set of N elements and we need to find the sum of the subsequence which:

- Has the maximum sum
- Is in Increasing order
- Has exactly K elements

For example:

Input: {9, -1, 2, 8, 10, -2, 20} and K = 3

In this, the subsequence satisfying our conditions of maximum sum and increasing order is:

{2, 8, 10} with sum = 20

{2, 8, 20} with sum = 30

{2, 10, 20} with sum = 32

{9, 10, 20} with sum = 39

And so on ...

The maximum sum subsequence satisfying the conditions is {9, 10, 20} with sum 39.

Note that in this problem, one fact changes that negative numbers can become a part of the answer.

Consider the case:

Input elements: {-1, -9, 5, 2, 10} and K = 3

In this case, our answer will be {-1, 5, 10} with sum 14. We had to take a negative number to satisfy the third condition on the number of elements.

Brute force approach

The brute force approach will be similar to the previous problem with one extra condition which can be taken care of in existing traversals.

The brute force approach is to generate all subsequences and for each subsequence, we need to check if the elements are in increasing order, of given size K and keep track of the largest sum.

For N elements, there will be $O(2^N)$ subsequences and to check the conditions, it would take $O(N)$ time for each subsequence.

With this, the time complexity will be $O(N \times 2^N)$ with constant space complexity $O(1)$.

The steps are:

- Generate all subsequences
- For each subsequence:
    - Check if it has the maximum sum, is in increasing order and consists of K elements
- Maximum sum is our answer

Note: We have covered the idea of generating all subsequences in previous problems (Hint: Use bit notation of integers)

Note: There is no viable Greedy Algorithm solution to this problem like the previous problem.

Dynamic Programming approach

The structure of our Dynamic Programming approach is as follows:

```
dp[i][j] = Sum of Longest sum subset with first
           i elements and length j with the jth
           element as the last element in the
           subsequence
```

The base case are as follows:

- If j (length of subsequence) is 0, then the answer is 0 as no element can be included.
- If i (considering first i elements) is 0, then the answer is 0 as no element is being considered for the answer.
- If j (length of subsequence) is 1, then the answer will be the ith element as one element needs to be included and i^{th} element should be the last element (based on our structure).

```
dp[i][0] = 0      ......    for all i from 0 to N
dp[0][j] = 0      ......    for all j from 0 to N
```

```
dp[i][1] = A[i] ……    for all i fron 0 to N
```

Think of the relation with which we can calculate the values.

The maximum sub sequence of size j with first i elements will be the maximum of all values that are of (size j-1 with any element among the first i-1 elements as the last element) + the ith element (as it should be the last element).

Understand this intuitively:

For size j with i^{th} element last element, if we remove the last element, we get:

A set of j-1 elements with the last element being one from the first i-1 elements. We need to find the maximum of this value in together with the addition of the ith element.

In the process, we need to ensure that the elements are in **increasing order**. The idea is we need to check that the ith element is greater than the last element of the smaller subsequence we are considering.

Note: You may think that the sum of ith element can be handled separately but this is not possible as the answer may include negative numbers.

Think about this point.

With this, our relation is as follows:

© **OpenGenus**

```
// Compute the relation
for i from 1 to N
    for j from 0 to i-1
        if (A[j] < A[i])
            for m from 1 to K (size)
                dp[i][l + 1] = MAXIMUM(dp[i][l
+ 1],
                                      dp[j][l] +
A[i])
```

The complete pseudocode is as follows:

```
array A of N elements, K (size)
N = length(A)
int dp[N][N]

// Base case
for i from 0 to N
    dp[i][0] = 0
    dp[0][i] = 0
    dp[i][1] = A[i]

// Compute the relation
for i from 1 to N
    for j from 0 to i-1
        if (A[j] < A[i])
            for m from 1 to K (size)
                dp[i][l + 1] = MAXIMUM(dp[i][l
+ 1],
                                      dp[j][l] +
A[i])
```

```
// Find the maximum value
answer = 0
for i from 0 to N
    if answer < dp[i][K]
        answer = dp[i][K]
```

With this, the complexity of our Dynamic Programming approach is as follows:

- Time complexity: $O(N^2)$
- Space complexity: $O(N^2)$

This is summarized by the following table:

Approach	Time Complexity	Space Complexity
Brute Force	$O(N \times 2^N)$	$O(1)$
Dynamic Programming	$O(N^2)$	$O(N^2)$

Note that how adding a condition that the subsequence should be of size K changed the following:

- Time complexity remained same $O(N^2)$
- Space complexity: Increased from $O(N)$ to $O(N^2)$

So, to summarize the impact of the last 4 problems, consider the following table for Dynamic Programming approaches:

Number	Approach	Time Complexity	Space Complexity
1	**Maximum Sum**	O(N)	O(N)
2	**#1 + size K**	$O(N^2)$	$O(N^2)$
3	**#1 + Increasing order**	$O(N^2)$	O(N)
4	**#3 + size K**	$O(N^2)$	$O(N^2)$

One interesting point to is that:

- If we add the condition of "**K elements**" to initial problem of Maximum Sum, the space complexity increases to $O(N^2)$.
- If we add the condition of "**Increasing order**" instead, the time complexity increases to $O(N^2)$.

So, limiting the problem size is related to time/ number of steps and specifying the order is related to the additional space required.

Hence, **limiting size** and **specifying order** are two opposite properties in terms of optimizations.

This results in a very interesting and challenging research problem in the domain of Algorithms. Think on this.

Maximum Sum Alternating Subsequence

In this problem, we are given a set of N elements and we need to find the sum of the largest subset with the maximum sum and has elements in alternating order (that is increasing and decreasing order one after another starting with decreasing order).

If a sequence $\{a_1, a_2, ..., a_N\}$ is in alternating order, then:

- $a_1 > a_2$
- $a_i > a_{i+1}$ if i is odd and i != 1
- $a_i < a_{i+1}$ if i is even

Example for our problem:

Input: $\{1, 9, -1, 2, 0, 1, 10\}$

The answer in this case is: $\{9, 2, 10\}$ with sum 21.

There are other subsequences which has more elements and following the alternating pattern but does not have the maximum sum. Such subsequences include:

- $\{1, -1, 2, 0, 1\}$
- $\{1, -1, 2, 1, 10\}$

And so on ...

Brute force approach

The brute force approach is to generate all subsequences and for each subsequence, we need to check if the elements are in alternating order and keep track of the largest sum.

For N elements, there will be $O(2^N)$ subsequences and to check the conditions, it would take $O(N)$ time for each subsequence.

With this, the time complexity will be $O(N \times 2^N)$ with constant space complexity $O(1)$.

The steps are:

- Generate all subsequences
- For each subsequence:
  - Check if it has the maximum sum and is in alternating order
- Maximum sum is our answer

Note: We have covered the idea of generating all subsequences in previous problems (Hint: Use bit notation of integers)

Like previous problems, there is no viable Greedy solution as a relative order is involved.

Dynamic Programming approach

This is a unique problem as we need two Dynamic Programming structure to solve this problem:

© **OpenGenus**

```
increase[i] = Sum of Maximum sum Alternating
              subsequence with A[i] being the
              last element and is greater than
              the previous element
```

```
decrease[i] = Sum of Maximum sum Alternating
              subsequence with A[i] being the
              last element and is less than the
              previous element
```

As you must have already thought by looking at the structures that a combination of the two is used to determine an alternating subsequence.

The base case is as follows:

```
increase[0] = A[0]

decrease[0] = A[0]
```

To arrive at the relation behind the structures, let us analyze the problem.

If we need to find increase[i] that is alternative subsequence which ends with the ith element and the ith element is greater (>) than the $(i-1)^{th}$ element.

As it is an alternative subsequence, we know that:

- $(i-1)^{th}$ element is less than $(i-2)^{th}$ element

This means that the answer for the first i-1 considered elements is captured by decrease[i-1]. Now, increase[i] needs to maximize its sum so it will be the maximum value of decrease[j] + A[i] where j >=0 and j < i.

This results in:

```
increase[i] = Maximum(decrease[j] + A[i])

            ...... for all j < i and A[i] > A[j]
```

Similarly, decrease[i] follow the same structure as related to increase[i].

If we need to find decrease [i] that is alternative subsequence which ends with the ith element and the ith element is less (<) than the $(i-1)^{th}$ element.

As it is an alternative subsequence, we know that:

- $(i-1)^{th}$ element is greater than $(i-2)^{th}$ element

This means that the answer for the first i-1 considered elements is captured by increase[i-1]. Now, decrease[i] needs to maximize its sum so it will be the maximum value of increase[j] + A[i] where j >=0 and j < i.

This results in:

```
decrease[i] = Maximum(increase[j] + A[i])

            ...... for all j < i and A[i] < A[j]
```

Once the values of increase[] and decrease[] has been calculated, we need to find the answer which is the maximum value across the two Dynamic Programming structure as we can end with any element.

```
Answer = Maximum(increase[i], decrease[i])
         ......  for all i
```

This covers the two components of the two Dynamic Programming structures:

```
for i from 0 to N-1
    for j from 0 to i-1
        if(A[i] > A[j])
            increase[i] = MAXIMUM(increase[i],
decrease[j] + A[i])
        else
```

```
            decrease[i] = MAXIMUM(decrease[i],
increase[j] + A[i])
```

The complete pseudocode is as follows:

```
increase[]
decrease[]

increase[0] = decrease[0] = A[0]

// Compute the recursive relation
for i from 0 to N-1
    for j from 0 to i-1
        if(A[i] > A[j])
            increase[i] = MAXIMUM(increase[i],
decrease[j] + A[i])
        else
            decrease[i] = MAXIMUM(decrease[i],
increase[j] + A[i])
    answer = MAXIMUM(answer, increase[i],
decrease[i])

We have the answer at this point
```

The complexity of this approach is as follows:

- Time complexity: $O(N^2)$
- Space complexity: $O(N)$

This table summarizes the complexity:

Approach	Time Complexity	Space Complexity
Brute Force	$O(N \times 2^N)$	$O(1)$
Dynamic Programming	$O(N^2)$	$O(N)$

Note that we added an additional condition to our previous problem "Maximum Sum Subsequence" with alternating order, the impact on complexity is as follows:

- Time complexity increased from $O(N)$ to $O(N^2)$
- Space complexity remained the same: $O(N)$

This property is consistent with our previous observations.

Longest Alternating Subsequence

We can view this problem in two ways:

- Replacing "sum" condition with "Alternating order" condition in the "Maximum Sum Problem"
- Removing "Sum" condition in the "Maximum Sum Alternating Subsequence"

In this problem, we are given a set of N elements and we need to find the sum of the largest subset which has elements in alternating order (that is increasing and decreasing order one after another starting with decreasing order).

If a sequence $\{a_1, a_2, ..., a_N\}$ is in alternating order, then:

- $a_1 > a_2$
- $a_i > a_{i+1}$ if i is odd and i != 1
- $a_i < a_{i+1}$ if i is even

Example for our problem:

Input: {1, 9, -1, 2, 0, 1, 10}

The answer in this case is: {1, -1, 2, 0, 1} with length 5.

There are other subsequences which has same or less number of elements and following the alternating pattern. Such subsequences include:

- {9, 2, 10}
- {1, -1, 2, 1, 10}

And so on ...

Brute force approach

The brute force approach is to generate all subsequences and for each subsequence, we need to check if the elements are in alternating order and keep track of the largest length.

For N elements, there will be $O(2^N)$ subsequences and to check the conditions, it would take $O(N)$ time for each subsequence.

With this, the time complexity will be $O(N \times 2^N)$ with constant space complexity $O(1)$.

The steps are:

- Generate all subsequences
- For each subsequence:
  - Check if it has the largest length and is in alternating order
- Maximum sum is our answer

Note: We have covered the idea of generating all subsequences in previous problems (Hint: Use bit notation of integers)

Like previous problems, there is no viable Greedy solution as a relative order is involved.

Dynamic Programming approach

This is a unique problem as we need two Dynamic Programming structure to solve this problem:

```
increase[i] = Length of the longest Alternating
              subsequence with A[i] being the
              last element and is greater than
              the previous element
```

```
decrease[i] = Length of the longest Alternating
              subsequence with A[i] being the
              last element and is less than the
              previous element
```

As you must have already thought by looking at the structures that a combination of the two is used to determine an alternating subsequence.

The base case is as follows:

```
increase[0] = 1; Considering: A[0]

decrease[0] = 1; Considering: A[0]
```

To arrive at the relation behind the structures, let us analyze the problem.

If we need to find increase[i] that is alternative subsequence which ends with the ith element and the ith element is greater (>) than the (i-1)^th element.

As it is an alternative subsequence, we know that:

- (i-1)^th element is less than (i-2)^th element

This means that the answer for the first i-1 considered elements is captured by decrease[i-1]. Now, increase[i] needs to maximize its length so it will be the maximum value of decrease[j] + 1 where j >=0 and j < i. 1 is for A[i].

This results in:

```
increase[i] = Maximum(decrease[j] + 1)
              // 1 for A[i]

              ...... for all j < i and A[i] > A[j]
```

Similarly, decrease[i] follow the same structure as related to increase[i].

If we need to find decrease [i] that is alternative subsequence which ends with the ith element and the ith element is less (<) than the (i-1)^th element.

As it is an alternative subsequence, we know that:

- $(i-1)^{th}$ element is greater than $(i-2)^{th}$ element

This means that the answer for the first i-1 considered elements is captured by increase[i-1]. Now, decrease[i] needs to maximize its length so it will be the maximum value of increase[j] + 1 where j >=0 and j < i.

This results in:

```
decrease[i] = Maximum(increase[j] + 1)
              // 1 for A[i]

              ...... for all j < i and A[i] < A[j]
```

Once the values of increase[] and decrease[] has been calculated, we need to find the answer which is the maximum value across the two Dynamic Programming structure as we can end with any element.

```
Answer = Maximum(increase[i], decrease[i])
          ......   for all i
```

This covers the two components of the two Dynamic Programming structures:

```
for i from 0 to N-1
    for j from 0 to i-1
        if(A[i] > A[j])
            increase[i] = MAXIMUM(increase[i],
decrease[j] + 1)
        else
            decrease[i] = MAXIMUM(decrease[i],
increase[j] + 1)
```

The complete pseudocode is as follows:

```
increase[]
decrease[]

increase[0] = decrease[0] = 1

// Compute the recursive relation
for i from 0 to N-1
    for j from 0 to i-1
        if(A[i] > A[j])
            increase[i] = MAXIMUM(increase[i],
decrease[j] + 1)
        else
            decrease[i] = MAXIMUM(decrease[i],
increase[j] + 1)
    answer = MAXIMUM(answer, increase[i],
decrease[i])

We have the answer at this point
```

The complexity of this approach is as follows:

- Time complexity: $O(N^2)$
- Space complexity: $O(N)$

This table summarizes the complexity:

Approach	Time Complexity	Space Complexity
Brute Force	$O(N \times 2^N)$	$O(1)$
Dynamic Programming	$O(N^2)$	$O(N)$

Note that we removed the sum condition for our previous problem "Maximum Sum Alternating Subsequence" but then, is no impact on the complexity.

The impact on complexity is as follows:

- Time complexity remained same: $O(N^2)$
- Space complexity remained same: $O(N)$

This property is consistent with our previous observations.

Optimizing relative order has more impact on complexity than optimizing Sum.

Newman Conway Sequence

Newman Conway Sequence is the sequence which follows a given recursive relation (p(n) = p(p(n-1)) + p(n-p(n-1))) to generate a series of numbers where p(n) is the nth number.

First few elements of Newman Conway Sequence are:

1 1 2 2 3 4 4 4 5 6 7 7........

In terms of mathematical model, the Newman Conway sequence follows the following Recurrence Relation:

```
P(n) = P(P(n - 1)) + P(n - P(n - 1))
where,
P(n) = n-th number in Newman Conway Sequence
with P(1) = P(2) = 1
```

We solve this using two approaches:

1. Naive approach $O(2^N)$ time
2. Dynamic Programming approach $O(N)$ time

Naive Approach

Implementing the Recurrence Relation as it is in the structure, following is the Pseudocode

```
unsigned int NewmanConwaySequenceTerm (unsigned int n)
{
    if(n == 1 or n == 2)
        return 1;
    else
```

```
NewmanConwaySequenceTerm(NewmanConwaySequenceTer
m(n - 1))
        + NewmanConwaySequenceTerm(n -
NewmanConwaySequenceTerm(n - 1));
}
```

Complexity

The Time and Space Complexities of code by using Naive
Approach are:

Time complexity: $O(2^N)$

Space complexity: k

space complexity here k means, k frames will loaded in RAM
containing the local variables declared in function with
respective data-type which will depend directly on architecture
of Operating System of Local Host Machine

Approach Using Dynamic Programming

Basic Idea in using Dynamic Programming is storing the
precomputed terms of a sequence in a data structure and use it
for next generating sequence term.

Algorithm

Step 1: Input to execute the following program is twofold, get
the positive input integer from user: the index of the required
Newman Conway Sequence term and the bool datatype second
input 'true' for generating the Newman Conway sequence till

75

the index provided by the user and 'false' for generating the particular Newman Conway sequence term.

Step 2: Check the requirement of the user against the Newman Conway Sequence by checking the status of flag whether it is 'true' or 'false'.

Step 3: If flag found 'true': generating the sequence, initializing the first three flagship members of the sequence as 0, 1 and 1 respectively in a data structure called array(in C++, any other linear data structure can be used in other languages) in size of n + 1.

Step 4: Further, computing the forward terms from pre-computer terms according to the recurrence relation. The advantage of using this approach is at each and every time computing higher indexed terms, we don't have to compute all the low indexed terms of sequence, which saves the resources (space and time).

Step 5: If flag found 'false': generating the required specific term, execute Step 3 and Step 4 with a slight change in way of displaying the output: return the positive integer situated at last index of the data structure used, is the required output.

Step 6: Stop.

The basic idea is as follows:

```
int ncs[n + 1];
// Base case
ncs[0] = 0;
ncs[1] = 1;
ncs[2] = 1;
// Bottom up dynamic programming approach
for (int i = 3; i <= n; i++)
```

```
ncs[i] = ncs[ncs[i - 1]] + ncs[i - ncs[i - 1]];
```

Following is the implementation of our Dynamic Programming
approach in C++:

```cpp
#include<iostream>
class NewmanConwaySequence
{
public:
    NewmanConwaySequence(unsigned int n) : n(n) {}
    void calculateNewmanConwaySequenceTermDP(bool
flag);
private:
    unsigned int n;
};
void
NewmanConwaySequence::calculateNewmanConwaySequenceTe
rmDP(bool flag)
{
    if(flag == true)
    {
        unsigned int ncs[n + 1];
        ncs[0] = 0;
        ncs[1] = 1;
        ncs[2] = 1;
        for (int i = 3; i <= n; i++)
            ncs[i] = ncs[ncs[i - 1]] + ncs[i - ncs[i -
1]];
        std::cout << "\nNewman Conway Sequence with "
<< n << " elements : ";
        for(int i = 1; i <= n; i++)
            std::cout << ncs[i] << " ";
    }
    else
    {
        unsigned int ncs[n + 1];
        ncs[0] = 0;
```

```cpp
        ncs[1] = 1;
        ncs[2] = 1;
        for (int i = 3; i <= n; i++)
            ncs[i] = ncs[ncs[i - 1]] + ncs[i - ncs[i -
1]];
        std::cout << "\nNewman Conway Sequence term at "
<< n << " indexed : ";
        std::cout << ncs[n];
    }
}
int main()
{
    unsigned int nValue, value;
    bool flag;
    std::cout << "\nEnter the Index of Newman Conway
Sequence : ";
    std::cin >> nValue;
    NewmanConwaySequence
aNewmanConwaySequenceoj(nValue);
    std::cout << "\nEnter the non-zero to generate the
Newman Conway Sequence or zero to generate particular term
in Newman Conway Sequence : ";
    std::cin >> value;
    if(value)
        flag = true;
    else
        flag = false;
    if(flag == true)

aNewmanConwaySequenceoj.calculateNewmanConwaySequence
TermDP(true);
    else

aNewmanConwaySequenceoj.calculateNewmanConwaySequence
TermDP(false);
 }
```

Input:

```
Enter the Index of Newman Conway Sequence: 12

Enter the non-zero to generate the Newman Conway
Sequence or zero to generate particular term in
Newman Conway Sequence: 1
```

Output:

```
Newman Conway Sequence with 12 elements:
1 1 2 2 3 4 4 4 5 6 7 7
```

Complexity

The Time and Space Complexities of code by using Dynamic Programming Approach are:

- Time complexity: O(N)
- Space complexity: O(N)

where n is the user required index of the Newman Conway Sequence.

Binomial Coefficient

Binomial Coefficient is the coefficient in the Binomial Theorem which is an arithmetic expansion. It is denoted as C(N, K) which is equal to N! / (K! * (N-K)!) where ! denotes factorial.

This follows a recursive relation using which we will calculate the N binomial coefficient in linear time O(N * K) using Dynamic Programming.

To know Binomial Coefficient, first we have to know what is Binomial Theorem?

What is Binomial Theorem?

Binomial Theorem is also called as Binomial Expansion delineate the powers in algebraic equations. Binomial Theorem helps us to find the expanded the expanded polynomial without multiplying the bunch of binomials at a time. The expanded polynomial will always contain one more than the power you are expanding.

Following figure shows the General formula to expand the algebraic equations by using Binomial Theorem,

$$(x + a)^n = \sum_{k=0}^{n} \binom{n}{k} x^k a^{n-k}$$

Where,

$\sum$ = Known as "Sigma Notation" used to sum all the terms in expansion from k = 0 to k = n

n = positive integer power of algebraic equation

$\binom{n}{k}$ = read as "n choose k"

According to theorem, expansion goes as following for any of the algebraic equation containing any positive power,

$$(x+y)^n = \binom{n}{0}x^n y^0 + \binom{n}{1}x^{n-1}y^1 + \binom{n}{2}x^{n-2}y^2 + \cdots + \binom{n}{n-1}x^1 y^{n-1} + \binom{n}{n}x^0 y^n$$

As after getting done by expansion one task remains pending that is to calculate the Binomial Coefficients (nCk)

Binomial Coefficients gives (nCk) combinations to choose k elements from n-element set.

How to calculate Binomial Coefficient?

Binomial coefficient (nCk) is calculated by computing according to following expansion,

$$C(n, k) = \frac{n!}{(n-k)! * k!}$$

As per the above expansion, Binomial Coefficients (nC0, nC1, nC2...nCn) of Binomial Theorem are computed.

Example:

3C2:

= 3! / ((3 - 2)! * 2!)

81

= 3! / (1! * 2!)

= 3! / (1 * 2)

= 3! / 2

= 6 / 2

The number of permutations on a set of n elements is given by n!

Note:

- 0! = 1
- 1! = 1

Naive Approach

The value of C(n,k) can be recursively calculated because of the only identity mentioned below :

```
C(n, k) = C(n-1, k-1) + C(n-1, k)
```

This holds true because:

```
C(n, k) = n! / (k! * (n-k)!)
        = (n-1)! * n / (k! * (n-k)!)
        = (n-1)! * n / ((k-1)! * k * (n-k-2)! *
(n-k-1) * (n-k))
```

```
         = (n-1)! / ((k-1)! * (n-k-1)!) * (n / k
* (n-k))
         = [(n-1)! / ((k-1)! * (n-k-1)!)] *
(1/(n-k) + 1/k)
         = (n-1)! / ((k-1)! * (n-k)!) + (n-1)! /
(k! * (n-k-1)!)
         = C(n-1, k-1) + C(n-1, k)
```

This has made the idea clear.

Note:

- C(n, 0) = 1
- C(n, n) = 1

The idea to implement the above recursive relation using a recursion function with base conditions. Following is the pseudocode:

```
int recursiveBinomialCoefficientMethod(int n,int k)
{
    if(k == n or k == 0)
        return 1;
    return (recursiveBinomialCoefficientMethod(n-1,k-
1)+recursiveBinomialCoefficientMethod(n-1,k));
}
```

Implementation of naïve approach in C++:

```
#include <iostream>
class BinomialCoefficient
```

83

```cpp
{
public:
    BinomialCoefficient(unsigned int n, unsigned int k) :
n(n), k(k) { }
    unsigned int recursiveBinomialCoefficientMethod(int n, int
k);
private:
    unsigned int n, k;
};
unsigned int BinomialCoefficient ::
recursiveBinomialCoefficientMethod(int n, int k)
{
    if(k == n or k == 0)
        return 1;
    return (recursiveBinomialCoefficientMethod(n - 1, k -
1) + recursiveBinomialCoefficientMethod(n - 1, k));
}
int main()
{
    unsigned int valueOfN, valueOfK;
    std::cout << "\nEnter the value of n : ";
    std::cin >> valueOfN;
    std::cout << "\nEnter the value of k : ";
    std::cin >> valueOfK;
    BinomialCoefficient aBinoCoeff(valueOfN, valueOfK);
    std::cout << "Value of C(" << valueOfN << "," <<
valueOfK << ") : " <<
aBinoCoeff.recursiveBinomialCoefficientMethod(valueOfN,
valueOfK);
}
```

Input:

```
Enter the value of n : 4
```

84

```
Enter the value of k : 2
```

Output:

```
Value of C(4, 2) : 6
```

Complexity

The Time and Space Complexities of code by using Naive Approach are:

Time complexity: $O(2^N)$

Space complexity: $O(K)$

In space complexity, k means, k frames will loaded in RAM containing the local variables declared in function with respective data-type which will depend directly on architecture of Operating System of Local Host Machine*

Approach Using Dynamic Programming

Basic Idea in using Dynamic Programming is implementing Pascal's Triangle.

Pascal's Triangle is the triangular arrangement of the binomial coefficients.

Algorithm

Step 1: Get the two inputs, the positive value of n and the non-positive value of k which denotes the k-th binomial coefficient in the Binomial Expansion.

Step 2: Allocate the array of size k + 1 with the value of 1 at 0th index and rest with value 0.

Step 3: Next, generating the sequence of pascal's triangle, with the first row containing single element valued 1 which was already created in step 2.

Step 4: Further next consecutive rows of pascal's triangle are computed from the previous row by adding the two consecutive elements, but step 4 is to be carried out upto k-times, for enclosing n-value times.

Step 5: Stop.

Implementation

```
#include <iostream>
class BinomialCoefficient
{
public:
    BinomialCoefficient(unsigned int n, unsigned int k) :
n(n), k(k) { }
    unsigned int DPBinomialCoefficientMethod(int n, int k);
private:
    unsigned int n, k;
};
unsigned int BinomialCoefficient ::
DPBinomialCoefficientMethod(int n, int k)
{
    unsigned int nCr[k + 1];
    for (int l = 0; l < k + 1; ++l)
        nCr[l] = 0;
    nCr[0] = 1;
    for (int p = 1; p <= n; p++)
```

86

```
    {
        for (int q = std::min(p, k); q > 0; q--)
            nCr[q] = nCr[q] + nCr[q - 1];
    }
    return nCr[k];
}
int main()
{
    unsigned int valueOfN, valueOfK;
    std::cout << "\nEnter the value of n : ";
    std::cin >> valueOfN;
    std::cout << "\nEnter the value of k : ";
    std::cin >> valueOfK;
    BinomialCoefficient aBinoCoeff(valueOfN, valueOfK);
    std::cout << "Value of C(" << valueOfN << "," <<
valueOfK << ") : " <<
aBinoCoeff.DPBinomialCoefficientMethod(valueOfN,
valueOfK);
}
```

Input:

```
Enter the value of n : 3
Enter the value of k : 2
```

Output:

```
Value of C(4, 2) : 3
```

Complexity

© **OpenGenus**

The Time and Space Complexities of code by using Dynamic Programming Approach are:

Time complexity: O(N * K)

Space complexity: O(K)

Permutation Coefficient

Given n and k, we will calculate permutation coefficient using dynamic programming in O(N * K) time complexity.

If we solve this problem using naive algorithm then time complexity would be exponential but we can reduce this to O(N * K) using Dynamic Programming. In this chapter, first of all we will visit the idea of Permutation coefficient, explore the naive approach and then, go into the dynamic programming approach to solve this efficiently.

What is Permutation Coefficient?

Permutation refers to the process of arranging all members of a given set to form a sequence. In case of permutation, order of elements is also considered.

To understand the permutation, let us take an example: Examine all the different ways in which a pair of objects can be selected from five distinguishable objects - A,B,C,D,E. If both the letters selected and order of selection are considered, then the following 20 outcomes are considered:

```
AB  BA  AC  CA  AD
DA  AE  EA  BC  CB
BD  DB  BE  EB  CD
DC  CE  EC  DE  ED
```

Each of these 20 possible selections is called a permutation. They can be called as permutations of five objects taken two at a time.

The number of permutations on a set of n elements is given by n!

here, n! = n * (n-1) * (n-2) ... 1

The permutation coefficient is represented by P(n,k). It is used to represent the number of ways to obtain an ordered subset of k elements from a set of n elements.

```
P(n,k)  =  n.(n-1).(n-2)...(n-k+1)

        =  n!/(n-k)!
```

P(n,k) = 1 if k=0

P(n,k) = 0 if k>n

Example:

P(5,2) = 5!/(5-2)!

= 5!/3!

= 5.4

= 20

Note

0! = 1

1! = 1

Naive Approach:

The value of P(n,k) can be recursively calculated using the below recursive formula:

```
P(n,k) = P(n-1, k) + k * P(n-1, k-1)
```

The idea to implement the above recursive relation using a recursion function with base conditions. Following is the pseudocode:

```
int permutationCoeff(int n,int k)
{
    if(k == 0) return 1;
    if(k > n) return 0;
    return (k*permutationCoeff(n-1,k-1)+permutationCoeff(n-1,k));
}
```

Implementation of Naive approach:

```
#include<bits/stdc++.h>
using namespace std;

//Returns value of P(n,k)
int permutationCoeff(int n,int k){
    //Base cases
    if(k==0){
        return 1;
    }
    if(k>n){
        return 0;
```

```
       }
       //Recursive call
       return  (k*permutationCoeff(n-1,k-1)+permutationCoeff(n-
1,k));
}

int main(){

    int  n=5,k=2;
    cout<<"Value of P("<<n<<", ""<<k<<") is
"<<permutationCoeff(n,k);
  return 0;
}
```

Output:

```
Value of P(5,2) is 20
```

Time Complexity of above code is $O(2^k)$

Basic Idea of using Dynamic Programming:

The above function is computing the same subproblems again and again. See the following recursive tree for n=5 and k=2:

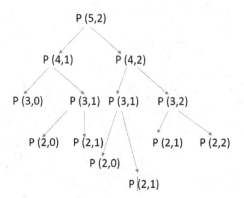

The function P(3,1) is called two times, P(2,1) is called three times. For large values of n, there will be many subproblems which are being called again and again. The re-computation of subproblems can be avoided by applying dynamic programming techniques.

To do this, we will compute permutation coefficient in a bottom-up manner and store all values in an array to avoid recursion calls.

Pseudocode:

```
int permutationCoeff(int n,int k)
{
    int  P[n+1][k+1];
    for(int  i=0;i<=n;i++)
    {
        for(int j=0;j<=min(i,k);j++)
        {
            if(j==0)  P[i][j]  =  1;
```

```
                    else        P[i][j] = P[i-1][j] + j * P[i-
1][j-1];
                    P[i][j+1]=0;
        }
    }
    return P[n][k];
}
```

Implementation of Dynamic Programming approach in C++:

```cpp
#include<bits/stdc++.h>
using namespace std;

//Returns value of P(n,k)
int permutationCoeff(int n,int k){

    int P[n+1][k+1];

    for(int i=0;i<=n;i++){
        for(int j=0;j<=min(i,k);j++){

                    //Base Cases
                    if(j==0){
                        P[i][j]=1;
                    }else{
                        P[i][j]=P[i-1][j]+j*P[i-1][j-1];
//calculating value using previously stored value.
                    }

                    P[i][j+1]=0;
        }
    }
    return P[n][k];
}

int main(){
```

```
    int n=5,k=2;
    cout<<"Value of P("<<n<<", ""<<k<<") is
"<<permutationCoeff(n,k);
  return 0;
}
```

Output:

```
Value of P(5,2) is 20
```

Complexity

Time Complexity is O(N * K)

(As two consecutive loops are running)

Space Complexity is O(N * K)

(To store the result, a 2D array is being used)

Nth Fibonacci number

A Fibonacci series is one in which every number is the sum of previous 2 numbers appearing in the series. The series goes something like: 0 1 1 2 3 5 8 13 21...

A number F_n, where n is the index of said number in the series is defined as $F_n = F_{n-1} + F_{n-2}$ for n>1 and the starting 2 terms of the series are fixed to F_0=0, F_1=1.

Fibonacci numbers find various uses in mathematics and computing so often that many a times these may go unnoticed. The Fibonacci series finds applications in algorithms like Fibonacci search technique, the Fibonacci heap data structure, graphs called Fibonacci cubes which are used to interconnect parallel & distributed systems.

Algorithm

Let the index of our required number be n.

In order to determine the number in Fibonacci sequence at nth position, we simply follow the premise:

$F_n = F_{n-1} + F_{n-2}$

For dynamic programming method, we need to store the previous series somewhere to arrive at the required Fn.

We make use of an array to perform our task.

Length of the array: N (Since we begin indexing from 0).

96

Now,

$F_0 = 0$

$F_1 = 1$

And for every position 'x' in the array, Fx = Fx-1 + Fx-2

So,

F2 = F1 + F0 = 1 + 0 = 1

F3 = F2 + F1 = 1 + 1 = 2

And so on.

Example

Let us take an example of 7th number in the series.

$$0 \ 1 \ 1 \ 2 \ 3 \ ...$$

We now have, n=7

In order to find the 7th number, we need to create an array of length n in order to store the entire series, since we begin from 0.

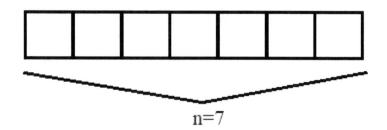

n=7

We now store every result a sum of values in previous 2 indices.

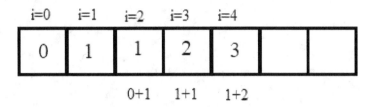

We get the last number from the array, which is our required result.

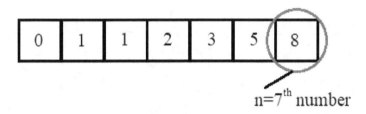

Thus, we divided this problem of the Nth number into n subproblems for numbers at every index and used the result of each in order to arrive at our final solution.

Pseudocode

```
function FibonacciNumber(index n):
        /*Create array of required length*/
        integer array FibArray[n+1]
        FibArray[0]=0
        FibArray[1]=1
```

```
        /*Loop over the array and calculate the numbers at
all positions*/
        for(i=2 to n+1)
                FibArray[i]=FibArray[i-
1]+FibArray[i-2]
        return FibArray[n+1]
```

Following is the implementation of the above approach in C++:

```cpp
//Function creates an array with specified length and returns
the last element as nth Fibonacci number
int fibonacciNumber(int n){
    int fibArray[n],i;
    fibArray[0] = 0, fibArray[1] = 1;
    for(i=0; i<n; i++)
        fibArray[i] = fibArray[i-1]+fibArray[i-2];
    return fibArray[n-1];
}

//The parameters in bracket may be ignored
//They are used to input command line arguments and are not
necessary
int main(int argc, char* argv){
    int n;
    cout<<"Which number in series do you want?";
    cin>>n;
    cout<<fibonacciNumber(n);
    return 0;
}
```

Space Optimization

The above solution stores all the previous numbers into the memory despite the fact that we need only the last number from this array. However, having to manually delete every element from our array just increases the time complexity of our program and is not efficient. We instead have another way, where we only make use of the last 2 results and replace the previous ones repeatedly with these. In this method, we do not have the requirement of an array to store our problem and instead simply calculate our solution in the same way as before with only the previous 2 numbers present every time.

Pseudocode:

```
function FibonacciNumber(index n):
        /*Store first 2 values of the sequence*/
        integer FibonacciFirst = 0, FibonacciSecond =
1, FibonacciResult
        /*Loop for n+1 times and replace the first and second
with values in the next indices*/
        for (i=2 to n+1)
                FibonacciResult = FibonacciFirst
+ FibonacciSecond
                FibonacciFirst = FibonacciSecond
                FibonacciSecond =
FibonacciResult
        return FibonacciResult
```

Following is the implementation in C++:

```cpp
//Function repeatedly iterates over the series till the specifed
point
int fibonacciNumber(int n){
    int i, fibonacciFirst = 0, fibonacciSecond = 1,
fibonacciResult;
    if(n == 0)
        return fibonacciFirst;
    else if(n == 1)
        return fibonacciSecond;
    else
        for(i=0; i<n; i++){
            fibonacciResult = fibonacciFirst +
fibonacciSecond;
            fibonacciFirst = fibonacciSecond;
            fibonacciSecond = fibonacciResult;
        }
    return fibonacciResult;
}

//The parameters in bracket may be ignored
//They are used to input command line arguments and are not
necessary
int main(int argc, char* argv){
    int n;
    cout<<"Which number in series do you want?";
    cin>>n;
    cout<<fibonacciNumber(n);
    return 0;
}
```

Complexity

- Worst case time complexity: $\Theta(n)$
- Average case time complexity: $\Theta(n)$
- Best case time complexity: $\Theta(n)$
- Space complexity: $\Theta(n)$
- Space optimized complexity: $\Theta(1)$

Applications

- Used in charting analysis (technical analysis) in stock trading along with trend lines and candlestick graphs.
- Conversion of miles to km (consecutive digits represent the nearest rounded value with left digit as miles and right as kilometers).
- Fibonacci cubes used for interconnecting parallel & distributed systems.
- Fibonacci heap data structure
- Fibonacci search technique

Longest Arithmetic Progression

The problem we will solve is that given a set of integers in sorted order, find length of longest arithmetic progression in that set. This can be solved by brute force in $O(N^3)$ while a dynamic programming approach with take $O(N^2)$ time complexity.

Arithmetic progression is set of numbers in which difference between two consecutive numbers is constant. Mathematical formula for arithmetic progression is

```
Tn = a + (n - 1) d where a is first element,
                T(n) is nth element and d is
constant.


1,2,3 is AP with d = 1
3,7,11,15 is AP with d = 4
```

Let's define in detail first. Our Problem statement is to find longest sequence of indices, $0 < i_1 < i_2 < \ldots < i_k < n$ such that sequence $A[i_1], A[i_2], \ldots, A[i_k]$ is an arithmetic progression.

Examples:

```
set[] = {1, 7, 10, 15, 27, 29}
```

```
output = 3
The longest arithmetic progression is {1, 15,
29}


set[] = {5, 10, 15, 20, 25, 30}
output = 6
 The longest arithmetic progression is {5, 10,
15, 20, 25, 30}
```

What will be the brute force solution?

A brute force solution is to one by one consider every pair as first two elements of AP and check for the remaining elements in sorted set. To consider all pairs as first two elements, we need to run a $O(N^2)$ nested loop. Inside the nested loops, we need a third loop which linearly looks for the more elements in Arithmetic Progression (AP). This process takes O(n3) time.

For better understanding, let us go through an example:

Let us consider a sorted array and we have to find 3 or more elements in AP. if we get 3 elements in AP we return TRUE otherwise FALSE.

In order to find three elements, we first fix an element as middle element and search for other two (one smaller and one greater). We start from the second element and fix every element as middle element. For an element set[j] to be middle of AP, there must exist elements 'set[i]' and 'set[k]' such that set[i] + set[k] = 2*set[j] where 0 <= i < j and j < k <=n-1.

We can follow this ALGO to find numbers:-

```
Initialize i as j-1 and k as j+1
Do following while i >= 0 and j <= n-1

If set[i] + set[k] is equal to 2*set[j], then we are
done.
If set[i] + set[k] > 2*set[j], then decrement i (do
i-).
Else if set[i] + set[k] < 2*set[j], then increment k
(do k++).
```

This will give answer to question if there exist three numbers in set which form AP.

If set contains two or more elements, minimum length of longest AP will be 2. **Why**? because any number will always form AP of length 2 with last element of set.

We can proceed with this problem using Dynamic Programming

The idea is to create a 2D table L[n][n]. An entry L[i][j] in this table stores Longest arithmetic progression with arr[i] and arr[j] as first two elements of AP and (j > i). The last column of the table is always 2 (as discussed above). Rest of the table is filled from bottom right to top left. To fill rest of the table, j (second element in AP) is first fixed. i and k are searched for a fixed j. If i and k are found such that i, j, k form an AP, then the value of L[i][j] is set as L[j][k] + 1. Note that the value of L[j][k] must have been filled before as the loop traverses from right to left columns.

Algorithm to find length of longest arithmetic progression

- For j = n L[i][j] = 2 for 0<i<n, bottom most column filled with 2.
- Fix j = n-1 to 1 and for each j do below steps:
- Find all i and k such that A[i], A[j] and A[k] form AP. Algorithm given above.
- Fill L[i][j] = 1 + L[j][k]
- Check if L[i][j] is longer than current max length, if yes, update it.
- Slight change for optimization, if A[i] + A[k] is greater than 2*A[j], we can safely fill L[i][j] as 2.
- While i > 0 even after k > n, fill all L[i][j] =2.

Example

Let us consider the example number 1 where input array was a[]={ 1, 3, 5, 6, 8, 7 }.

Now when we will build the dp[n][n] matrix it would look like following-

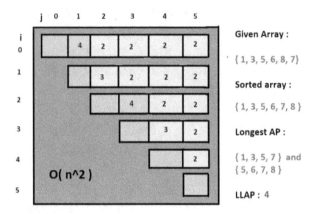

From the above method we can see that we will be using only n-1 + ... + 3 + 2 + 1 space of the matrix making the time complexity to be n*(n-1)/2 ~ $O(N^2)$.

Complexity

Time Complexity: $O(N^2)$ [Dynamic programming]

Auxiliary Space: $O(N^2)$

Implementation in C++

```cpp
#include <iostream>
using namespace std;
// Returns length of the longest AP subset in a given set
int lenghtOfLongestAP(int set[], int n)
{
    if (n &lt;= 2)    return n;
    // Create a table and initialize all values as 2. The value of
    // L[i][j] stores LLAP with set[i] and set[j] as first two
```

```
        // elements of AP. Only valid entries are the entries where
j>i
    int L[n][n];
    int llap = 2;    // Initialize the result
    // Fill entries in last column as 2. There will always be
    // two elements in AP with last number of set as second
    // element in AP
    for (int i = 0; i < n; i++)
        L[i][n-1] = 2;
    // Consider every element as second element of AP
    for (int j=n-2; j>=1; j--)
    {
        // Search for i and k for j
        int i = j-1, k = j+1;
        while (i >= 0 && k <= n-1)
        {
            if (set[i] + set[k] < 2*set[j])
                k++;

            // Before changing i, set L[i][j] as 2
            else if (set[i] + set[k] > 2*set[j])
            {   L[i][j] = 2, i--;    }

            else
            {
                // Found i and k for j, LLAP with i and j as
first two
                // elements is equal to LLAP with j and k as
first two
                // elements plus 1. L[j][k] must have been
filled
                // before as we run the loop from right side
                L[i][j] = L[j][k] + 1;

                // Update overall LLAP, if needed
                llap = max(llap, L[i][j]);

                // Change i and k to fill more L[i][j] values for
                // current j
                i--; k++;
```

```
                }
        }
}
        // If the loop was stopped due to k becoming more
than
        // n-1, set the remaining entties in column j as 2
        while (i >= 0)
        {
            L[i][j] = 2;
            i--;
        }
    }
    return llap;
}
int main()
{
    int set1[] = {1, 7, 10, 13, 14, 19};
    int n1 = sizeof(set1)/sizeof(set1[0]);
    cout << lenghtOfLongestAP(set1, n1) << endl;
    return 0;
}
```

Output:

4

Number of arithmetic progression subsequences

Given an array of n positive integers. The task is to count the number of Arithmetic Progression subsequence in the array.

Arithmetic Progression is defined as a series of a, a + d, a + 2 * d, etc.

By difference of Arithmetic Progression, we mean d.

Let us look at few of Examples:

```
Input : arr[] = { 1, 2, 3 }
Output : 8
Arithmetic Progression subsequence from the
given array are: {}, { 1 }, { 2 }, { 3 }, { 1,
2 },
 { 2, 3 }, { 1, 3 }, { 1, 2, 3 }.


Input : arr[] = { 10, 20, 30, 45 }
Output : 12


Input : arr[] = { 1, 2, 3, 4, 5 }
Output : 23
```

Note: 1.Empty sequence or single element sequence is Arithmetic Progression.

2.we have considered A[i] in range 1 to 1000000(inclusive).

Since empty sequence and single element sequence is also arithmetic progression, so we initialize the answer with n (number of elements in the array) + 1.

Now, we need to find the arithmetic progression subsequence of length greater than or equal to 2. Let minimum and maximum of the array be minarr and maxarr respectively. Observe, in all the arithmetic progression subsequences, the range of common difference will be from (minarr − maxarr) to (maxarr − minarr).

We will solve this problem by dynamic programming. Let dp[i] denote the number of AP's ending at i and having difference equal to d. So, if our current number is equal to A[i], we need to find all the positions j < i such that A[j] = A[i] - diff and we will take sum of dp[j] for those j's. It is equivalent to extending the APs ending at position j with the element at position i.

```
Hence dp[i] = sum_(j = 1 to i - 1) dp[j]
    such that A[j] = A[i] - diff
```

we can optimize this by maintaining a sum array where sum[x] will record sum of all the DP's where the value of array elements was x.

```
sum[x] = sum of all dp[i]'s
```

```
such that A[i] = x.
```

After this, our dp will be.

```
Hence dp[i] = sum[A[i] - diff] + 1.
```

Now with this optimization, our DP computation will take O(N) time.

Complexity

Time complexity: O(N)

Space Complexity: O(N)

Implementation

Let us look at Dynamic programming approach:

```cpp
#include<bits/stdc++.h>
#define MAX 1000001
using namespace std;
int numofAP(int a[], int n)
{
    // initializing the minimum value and
    // maximum value of the array.
    int minarr = INT_MAX, maxarr = INT_MIN;
    // Finding the minimum and maximum
    // value of the array.
    for (int i = 0; i < n; i++)
```

```
{
        minarr = min(minarr, a[i]);
        maxarr = max(maxarr, a[i]);
}
// dp[i] is going to store count of APs ending
// with arr[i].
// sum[j] is going to store sun of all dp[]'s
// with j as an AP element.
int dp[n], sum[MAX];
// Initialize answer with n + 1 as single elements
// and empty array are also DP.
int ans = n + 1;
// Traversing with all common difference.
for (int d=(minarr-maxarr); d<=(maxarr-minarr); d++)
{
        memset(sum, 0, sizeof sum);
        // Traversing all the element of the array.
        for (int i = 0; i < n; i++)
        {
                // Initialize dp[i] = 1.
                dp[i] = 1;
                // Adding counts of APs with given differences
                // and a[i] is last element.
                // We consider all APs where an array element
                // is previous element of AP with a particular
                // difference
                if (a[i] - d >= 1 && a[i] - d <= 1000000)
                        dp[i] += sum[a[i] - d];
                ans += dp[i] - 1;
                sum[a[i]] += dp[i];
        }
}
return ans;
}
// Driver code
int main()
{
    int arr[] = { 1, 2, 3 };
    int n = sizeof(arr)/sizeof(arr[0]);
```

```
        cout << numofAP(arr, n) << endl;
        return 0;
}
```

Output:

8

Longest Bitonic Subsequence

The problem we will solve is given a sequence an array of positive integers and have to find the length of longest bitonic subsequence. Using dynamic programming ideas, we will solve this on O(N^2) time complexity

A bitonic sequence is a sequence which is first increasing to a peak value and then decreasing that is it is of the following form:

```
x1, x2, x3, ... xn
where:
    x1 < x2 < x3 < ... < xm
    xm > xm+1 > xm+2 > ... > xn
```

For example:

```
10, 25, 36, 40, 59, 48, 34, 20, 5

Here the sequence first increases from 10 to 59
then descreases to 5.
```

Note:

An increasing order sequence is considered Bitonic with the decreasing part as empty

A decreasing order sequence is considered Bitonic with the increasing part as empty.

EXAMPLES:

```
arr[] = {1, 11, 2, 10, 4, 5, 2, 1}
 the longest bitonic sequence is 1, 2, 4, 5, 2,
1 of length 6.
arr[] = {0, 8, 4, 12, 2, 10, 6, 14, 1, 9, 5, 13,
3, 11, 7, 15}
The longest bitonic sequence is 0, 8, 12, 14, 13,
11, 7 of length 7.
```

```
LIS     peak    LDS
 |       |       |
 |       v       |
 |      14       |
 v   12     13   v
    8          11
    0           7
```

Note that a bitonic sequence starting from a value reaches a peak value in a strict increasing order of values. Then it starts decreasing monotonically. So, we can easily perceive that a bitonic sequence consists of a increasing subsequence and a decreasing subsequence. So, a longest bitonic subsequence would be subsequence that consists of a longest increasing subsequence (LIS) ending at peak and a longest decreasing subsequence (LDS) starting at peak.

So, the longest bitonic subsequence with peak at a position i would consists of longest increasing subsequence that ends at i and a longest decreasing subsequence starting at i. We need to construct two arrays LIS[] and LDS[] such that for each position i.

LIS[i]: length of the Longest Increasing subsequence ending at arr[i].

LDS[i]: length of the longest Decreasing subsequence starting from arr[i].

LIS[i]+LDS[i]-1: the length Longest Bitonic Subsequence with peak at i.

We need to find the position i with maximum value of LIS[i]+LDS[i]-1.

In order to find solution of biotonic subsequence we can use the complete logic of Longest Increasing Subsequence, You may revisit previous chapter on longest increasing subsequence for better understanding.

Example walk-through

Let us take an example:

```
arr[]= {1, 11, 2, 10, 4, 5, 2, 1}
```

for this we need to find two new array LIS[] (longest increasing subsequence) and LDS[] (longest decreasing subsequence)

For LIS[i]:-

```
LIS[0] = {1}
LIS[i] = {Max(LIS[j])} + 1 where j < i and
arr[j] < arr[i]
         = arr[i], if there is no such j
```

Initial value:

LIS[]:

array	1	11	2	10	4	5	2	1
value	1	1	1	1	1	1	1	1

Final value:

LIS[]:-

array	1	11	2	10	4	5	2	1

| value | 1 | 2 | 2 | 3 | 3 | 4 | 2 | 1 |

For LDS[]:-

```
LDS[n] = {1}
LDS[i] = 1+ {Max(LDS[j])} where j > i and arr[j]
< arr[i]
         = arr[i], if there is no such j
```

Here, we used the method of finding LIS[] in reverse order, let us see how.

Algorithm

```
/* Compute LDS values from right to left */
For (i = n-2; i >= 0; i-- )
   For (j = n-1; j > i; j--)
       If(arr[i] > arr[j]  && lds[i] < lds[j] +1)
           Lds[i] = lds[j] +1;
```

Step 1:
LDS[]:

| index | 1 | 2 | 3 | 4 | 5 | 6 | i=7 | j=8 |

119

array	1	11	2	10	4	5	2	1
value	1	1	1	1	1	1	1	1

Step 2:-
LDS[]:-

index	1	2	3	4	5	i=6	7	j=8
array	1	11	2	10	4	5	2	1
value	1	1	1	1	1	1	2	1

LDS[]:-

index	1	2	3	4	5	i=6	j=7	8
array	1	11	2	10	4	5	2	1
value	1	1	1	1	1	2	2	1

Step 3:-
LDS[]:-

index	1	2	3	4	i=5	6	7	j=8
array	1	11	2	10	4	5	2	1
value	1	1	1	1	1	3	2	1

LDS[]:-

index	1	2	3	4	i=5	6	j=7	8
array	1	11	2	10	4	5	2	1
values	1	1	1	1	2	3	2	1

LDS[]

120

index	1	2	3	4	i=5	j=6	7	8
array	1	11	2	10	4	5	2	1
value	1	1	1	1	3	3	2	1

Similarly, we can repeat the procedure for rest value of **LDS[i]** and get a final result as shown:
LDS[]:-

array	1	11	2	10	4	5	2	1
value	1	5	2	4	3	3	2	1

Our final value in list is given as:
LIS[]

array	1	11	2	10	4	5	2	1
value	1	2	2	3	3	4	2	1

LDS[]

array	1	11	2	10	4	5	2	1
value	1	5	2	4	3	3	2	1

LIS[]+LDS[]-1

array	1	11	2	10	4	5	2	1
value	1	6	3	6	5	6	3	1

Final value in finding Bitonic sequence can be given as:-

Input: {1,11,2,10,4,5,2,1}
Output: 6
LIS[]+LDS[]-1

array	1	11	2	10	4	5	2	1
value	1	*6*	3	*6*	5	*6*	3	1

Longest Bitonic Subsequence is of length 6.

Below is C++ implementation of above idea:

```cpp
#include<iostream>
using namespace std;
// Utility function to print Longest Bitonic
// Subsequence
void print(vector<int>& arr, int size)
{
    for(int i = 0; i < size; i++)
        cout << arr[i] << " ";
}
// Function to construct and print Longest
// Bitonic Subsequence
void printLBS(int arr[], int n)
{
    // LIS[i] stores the length of the longest
    // increasing subsequence ending with arr[i]
    vector<vector<int>> LIS(n);
    // initialize LIS[0] to arr[0]
    LIS[0].push_back(arr[0]);
    // Compute LIS values from left to right
    for (int i = 1; i < n; i++)
    {
        // for every j less than i
        for (int j = 0; j < i; j++)
        {
```

```cpp
        if ((arr[j] < arr[i]) &&
            (LIS[j].size() > LIS[i].size()))
            LIS[i] = LIS[j];
    }
    LIS[i].push_back(arr[i]);
}
/* LIS[i] now stores Maximum Increasing
   Subsequence of arr[0..i] that ends with
   arr[i] */
// LDS[i] stores the length of the longest
// decreasing subsequence starting with arr[i]
vector<vector<int>> LDS(n);
// initialize LDS[n-1] to arr[n-1]
LDS[n - 1].push_back(arr[n - 1]);
// Compute LDS values from right to left
for (int i = n - 2; i >= 0; i--)
{
    // for every j greater than i
    for (int j = n - 1; j > i; j--)
    {
        if ((arr[j] < arr[i]) &&
            (LDS[j].size() > LDS[i].size()))
            LDS[i] = LDS[j];
    }
    LDS[i].push_back(arr[i]);
}
// reverse as vector as we're inserting at end
for (int i = 0; i < n; i++)
    reverse(LDS[i].begin(), LDS[i].end());
/* LDS[i] now stores Maximum Decreasing Subsequence
   of arr[i..n] that starts with arr[i] */
int max = 0;
int maxIndex = -1;
for (int i = 0; i < n; i++)
{
    // Find maximum value of size of LIS[i] + size
    // of LDS[i] - 1
    if (LIS[i].size() + LDS[i].size() - 1 > max)
    {
```

```
            max = LIS[i].size() + LDS[i].size() - 1;
            maxIndex = i;
        }
    }
    // print all but last element of LIS[maxIndex] vector
    print(LIS[maxIndex], LIS[maxIndex].size() - 1);
    // print all elements of LDS[maxIndex] vector
    print(LDS[maxIndex], LDS[maxIndex].size());
}
// Driver program
int main()
{
    int arr[] = { 1, 11, 2, 10, 4, 5, 2, 1 };
    int n = sizeof(arr) / sizeof(arr[0]);
    printLBS(arr, n);
    return 0;
}
```

Output

```
1 11 10 5 2 1
```

Complexity

Time complexity of above Dynamic Programming solution is $O(N^2)$.

Auxiliary space used by the program is $O(N^2)$.

Maximum Sum Bitonic Subsequence

The problem we are solving is that: Given a sequence of numbers in an array A[0.......N]. Find the sum of the maximum bitonic subsequence in the array.

This if approached using a naive algorithm will take exponential time O(N * 2^N) but we can reduced it to O(N^2) using Dynamic programming. We will visit the idea of bitonic sequence, explore the naive approach and then, go into the dynamic programming technique to solve this efficiently.

What is a Bitonic subsequence?

A subsequence in an array which first increases and then decreases.

Example:

A[]={5, 10, 16, 45, 32, 100, 10, 16, 9}

The bitoni subsequences are-:

{5,10,16,32,16,9}

{10,16,45,100,10,9}

{16,32,100,10,9}

and so on....

Maximum sum bitonic subsequence means the bitonic subsequence whose sum is maximum.

In the given example that bitonic subsequence is-:

{5,10,16,45,100,16,9}

And Sum=201.

For other subsequences, the sum of elements will be less than 201.

Naive approach

The naive approach involves:

- Generating all subsequences (takes $O(2^N)$ time complexity to generate all 2^N subsequences) (can be done using bitmap)
- For each subsequence:
    - Check if it is a bitonic sequence (taken $O(N)$ time complexity)
    - If it is a bitonic sequence, take the sum and check if it is large than the previously recorded sum

This way we can find the maximum sum bitonic subsequence in $O(N * 2^N)$ time complexity.

With Dynamic programming, we can reduce this to $O(N^2)$ time complexity.

Basic Idea of using Dynamic Programming

We are going to use Dynamic Programming approach to solve this problem.

We have to maintain two arrays namely:

- MSB[i] indicates the maximum sum of increasing bitonic subsequence ending at element A[i]
- MSD[i] indicates the sum of decreasing bitonic subsequence starting at A[i].

Once we have maintained these two arrays, we find the Maximum sum bitonic subsequence by finding maximum of MSB[i] + MSD[i] - Array[i] for all i.

```
Maximum sum bitonic subsequence =
        max(MSB[i]+MSD[i]-Arr[i])
```

Pseudocode

Initialize MSB and MSD with the initial values:

```
for (int i = 0; i < n; i++)
{
    MSB[i] = arr[i];
    MSD[i] = arr[i];
}
```

Calculate MSB values:

```
// Compute MSB values from left to right
```

```
for (int i = 1; i < n; i++)
{
    for (int j = 0; j < i; j++)
    {

            if (arr[i] > arr[j] && MSB[i] < MSB[j] +
arr[i])

            MSB[i] = MSB[j] + arr[i];
    }
 }
```

Calculate MSD values:

```
// Compute MSD values from right to left
for (int i = n - 2; i >= 0; i--)
{
    for (int j = n - 1; j > i; j--)
    {
        if (arr[i] > arr[j] && MSD[i] < MSD[j] + arr[i])
        MSD[i] = MSD[j] + arr[i];
    }
}
```

Calculate the final maximum value using MSB and MSD:

```
// Find the maximum value of MSB[i] + MSD[i] - arr[i]
for (int i = 0; i < n; i++)
{
    max = max(max, (MSD[i] + MSB[i] - arr[i]));
}
```

C++ Implementation

Following is the complete C++ implementation:

```cpp
#include <bits/stdc++.h>
    using namespace std;

    // Function return maximum sum of Bi-tonic sub-sequence
    int MaxSum(int arr[], int n)
{

    int max = INT_MIN;

    // MSB[i]-: Maximum sum Increasing Bi-tonic
    // subsequence ending with arr[i]
    // MSD[i]-: Maximum sum Decreasing Bi-tonic
    // subsequence starting with arr[i]
    int MSB[n], MSD[n];
    for (int i = 0; i < n; i++)
    {
        MSB[i] = arr[i];
        MSD[i] = arr[i];
    }

    // Compute MSB values from left to right
    for (int i = 1; i < n; i++)
    {
        for (int j = 0; j < i; j++)
        {

                if (arr[i] > arr[j] && MSB[i] < MSB[j]
+ arr[i])

                    MSB[i] = MSB[j] + arr[i];

        }
    }

    // Compute MSD values from right to left
    for (int i = n - 2; i >= 0; i--)
    {
```

```
            for (int j = n - 1; j > i; j--)
            {
                if (arr[i] > arr[j] && MSD[i] < MSD[j] +
arr[i])
                MSD[i] = MSD[j] + arr[i];
            }
        }

    // Find the maximum value of MSB[i] + MSD[i] - arr[i]
    for (int i = 0; i < n; i++)
    {
        max = max(max, (MSD[i] + MSB[i] - arr[i]));
    }

    // return max sum of bi-tonic sub-sequence
    return max;
    }


    int main()
    {
    int A[] = {5, 10, 16, 45, 32, 100, 10, 16, 9 };
    int n = sizeof(A) / sizeof(A[0]);
    cout << "Maximum Sum Bitonic Subsequence : " <<
MaxSum(A, n);

    return 0;
    }
```

Output:

```
Maximum Sum Bitonic Subsequence : 201
```

Time and Space Complexity

The above approach uses Dynamic Programming and hence a nested loop so complexity is $O(N^2)$ where N is the input size.

Space Complexity: $O(N)$

Find if a Subset with sum divisible by m exist

In this problem we will be given an array of size n and a number m and we have to find whether there exists a subset with sum divisible by m.

Example

Consider the following set S:

```
{ 2, 4, 6, 11, 2}
```

There exists no subset which is divisible by 7

At the same time, we have multiple subsets that is divisible by 4

```
{2, 2} {4} {2, 4, 2} {2, 6} {2, 4, 6}
```

We solve this using two approaches:

- Naive algorithm $O(2^N)$
- Dynamic Programming $O(N * M)$

Naive Algorithm

Basic Idea:

Generate all possible subset sum using recursion or iteratively and check if the current sum is divisible by m.

If we visualize this method by making a recursive tree, we see that there will be redundant cases and thus the complexity is exponential.

Pseudocode of Naive algorithm

```
void subsetSums(int arr[], int l, int r,
int sum=0)
{
    // Check current subset
    if (l > r)
    {
        if(sum%m==0&&sum!=0)
        return  true;
    }

    // Subset including arr[l]
    subsetSums(arr, l+1, r, sum+arr[l]);

    // Subset excluding arr[l]
    subsetSums(arr, l+1, r, sum);
    return  false;
}
```

Time Complexity

Since we generate all possible subset sums, and there are 2^N subsets in totality, therefore complexity of the naive algorithm is $O(2^N)$ where n is the number of elements in the array.

Efficient Algorithm using Dynamic Programming

Basic Idea:

We will use Dynamic Programming approach to solve this problem efficiently.

Here we take two cases:

- n>m-For all such cases, there will always be a subset divisible by m which we can easily prove by using pigeonhole principle.
- n<=m: For all such cases we create an array DP[] of size m which is of type bool . We initialize that array with false. This array gives the status of all possible sum modulo m.

```
DP[i] = true if subset with sum S modulo m = i
        exists
```

We use another array temp store all the new encountered sum (after modulo). It is used to make sure that arr[i] is added only to those entries for which DP[j] was true before current iteration.

Algorithm

We loop through all the elements in the given array and for each element arr[i] we check that if DP[j]==true we mark DP[(j+arr[i]) modulo m]=true and temp[(j+arr[i]) modulo m]=true which denotes that a subset with sum exist whose modulus with m gives the value j.

```
if DP[j] == true and for each arr[i]
```

```
   set DP[ (j+arr[i])%m ] = true
   set temp[ (j+arr[i])%m ] = true
```

After that we update the DP[j]=true if temp[j]=true. In the beginning of every iteration we check if DP[0]=true, if that is the case we return true which means a subset sum exists whose modulus with m gives the value 0.

```
if temp[i] = true
    set DP[i] = true
```

```
DP[0] is our answer
```

Pseudocode:

```
boolSubsetSum(int arr[])
{
  initialize DP[] with false;
  if(DP[0]==true)
    return true;

  for(i=0;i<size;i++)
  {
    initialize temp[] with false;
    for(j=0;j<m;j++)
    {
        if(DP[j]==true)
```

```
            {
                if(DP[(j+arr[i])%m]==false)
                {
                    temp[(j+arr[i])%m]=true;
                }
            }
        }
        for(i=0;i<m;i++)
        {
            if(temp[j]==true)
                DP[j]=true;
        }
        DP[arr[i]%m] = true;
    }
    return DP[0];
}
```

C++ Implementation:

Following is the C++ implementation:

```
#include <bits/stdc++.h>
using namespace std;

bool modularSum(int arr[], int n, int m)
{
    //According to Pigeonhole Principle
    if (n > m)
        return true;

    //DP[] array keeps track of all possible
    //subset sum modulo m
    bool DP[m];
    memset(DP, false, m);

    for (int i=0; i<n; i++)
```

```
    {
        //if DP[0]==true that means
        //A subset with sum divisible by m exists
        if (DP[0])
            return true;

        // To store all the new encountered sum
(after
        // modulo). It is used to make sure that
arr[i]
        // is added only to those entries for which
DP[j]
        // was true before current iteration.
        bool temp[m];
        memset(temp,false,m);

        //For each element in arr[] we find if
        //DP[j] exists and calculate next possible
        //value of sum modulus m
        for (int j=0; j<m; j++)
        {
            if (DP[j] == true)
            {
                if (DP[(j+arr[i]) % m] == false)

                    //Update temp
                    temp[(j+arr[i]) % m] = true;
            }
        }

        // Updating all the elements of temp to
DP
        for (int j=0; j<m; j++)
                if (temp[j])
                        DP[j] = true;

        //Since single element sum is also
possible
        DP[arr[i]%m] = true;
    }
```

```
    return DP[0];
}


int main()
{
int arr[] = {2,4,2,1,5};
int n = sizeof(arr)/sizeof(arr[0]);
int m = 9;

modularSum(arr, n, m) ? cout << "YES\n" :

        cout << "NO\n";

    return 0;
}
```

Output:

YES

Time Complexity:

Since the outer loop is executing n times and for each iteration of outer loop, the inner loop executes m times, the complexity becomes O(NM) where n is the number of array elements and m is the divisor.

Fibonacci Series in Reverse Order

In Fibonacci series each number is the sum of 2 preceding ones starting from 0 and 1.

F(0) = 0, F(1) = 1,and F(n) = F(n-1)+F(n-2) for n>1

A key point to note here is that as Fibonacci number depends on previous Fibonacci numbers, we have to generate it in forward pass that is in order. Instead of printing it directly, we can delay it to print it in reverse order.

Naive Approach

In this approach, we keep on storing Fibonacci numbers by computing them using the recurrence relation and once we have reached our goal, we print the Fibonacci array in reverse.

The function fib(n) simply returns the sum of fib(n-1) and fib(n-2) which then recurse and keep summing values until they reach base cases.

Code:

```cpp
#include <iostream>
#include <vector>
using namespace std;
int fib(int n){
    if(n == 0)return 0;
    else if(n == 1)return 1;
```

```
        return fib(n-1) + fib(n - 2);
}
int main () {

    int n = 10;
    std::vector<int> V; // vector to store the
Fibonacci numbers.

    V.push_back(0); // fib(0) = 0
    V.push_back(1); // fib(1) = 1

    for(int i=2; i<=n; i++) {
        V.push_back(fib(i)); // fib(i) = fib(i-
1)+fib(i-2);
    }
    // reversing the vector to get required series
    int l = 0, r = V.size()-1;
    while(l<r){
        swap(V[l],V[r]);
        l++;
        r--;
    }
    // printing the Fibonacci series in reverse
order
    for(int element: V){
        std::cout<<element<<" ";
    }

    return 0;
}
```

fib(int n) is the function that computes Fibonacci number. It handles 2 edge cases when n == 1 and n == 0, all the other values of n are computed using the recurrence relation.

Time Complexity:

$$T(n) = T(n-1) + T(n-2) + O(1)$$

The above time complexity relation is derived from the recurrence relation where to calculate fib(n) we first compute fib(n-1) and fib(n-2) and perform an addition of O(1) time.

The overall complexity thus becomes $O(2^N)$ which is termed as exponential.

Dynamic Programming

Dynamic Programming is an algorithmic technique in which the key idea is to store the values of smaller problems such that in case, the value is required again, it will return the value instead of recomputing. This works in problems which can be broken into smaller problems and smaller problems are encountered multiple times. When applicable, dynamic programming can reduce time complexity greatly.

One key observation we can make in the naive approach described above is that to compute fib(n) we call fib(n-1) and fib(n-2), later to compute fib(n-1) we call fib(n-2) and fib(n-3), as we can see fib(n-2) is being called twice even though its return value remains the same for both the function calls, which as explained is the perfect scenario for us to use dynamic programming.

Recursive DP

Assume fib[i] represents i^{th} Fibonacci number and to compute this we need two previous values namely fib[i-1] and fib[i-2], if

141

we create a check for each function call to check if some other function call has already answered this query then we can just return this number from the memo table in O(1) time without having to recalculate it.

```
fib[i] = fib[i-1] + fib[i-2]
```

Below is the code for the above-discussed approach.

Pseudocode:

```
function Fibonacci(index i, array &memo):
        if(i == 0) return 0
    if(i == 1) return 1
    if(memo[i] != null) return memo[i];
    memo[i] = Fibonacci(i-1, memo) + Fibonacci(i -
2, memo)
    return memo[i]
```

Implementation in C++:

```
#include <iostream>
#include <vector>
using namespace std;
int fib(int n, vector<int> &dp){
    if(n == 0)return 0;
    else if(n == 1)return 1;
    if(dp[n])return dp[n];
    dp[n] = fib(n-1) + fib(n - 2);
    return dp[n];
}
int main () {
```

```cpp
    int n = 10;
    std::vector<int> V; // vector to store the
Fibonacci numbers.
    std::vector<int> dp(n+1,0); //Memo table
    V.push_back(0); // fib(0) = 0
    V.push_back(1); // fib(1) = 1

    for(int i=2; i<=n; i++) {
        V.push_back(fib(i,dp)); // fib(i) = fib(i-
1)+fib(i-2);
    }
    // reversing the vector to get required series
    int l = 0, r = V.size()-1;
    while(l<r){
        swap(V[l],V[r]);
        l++;
        r--;
    }
    // printing the Fibonacci series in reverse
order
    for(int element: V){
        std::cout<<element<<" ";
    }

    return 0;
}
```

Time Complexity:

T(N) = O(N)

We never compute any Fibonacci number more than once and
to compute any number we perform either vector lookups of
precomputed Fibonacci numbers or compute them once, hence
our overall time complexity becomes O(n).

Dry run:

This is how our function call tree will look like when we call fib(6).

those red crosses represent the function calls that didn't calculate the Fibonacci value and returned precomputed values from memo table instead.

Iterative DP

Even though the recursive DP seems like a great leap in time complexity optimization but there is still a problem with it.

Function call overhead is constant time factor compilers take to process which function to call before actually executing the function itself, hence if possible iterative code is preferred over recursive ones whenever possible as they generally perform better.

In this approach, we initialize fib[0] and fib[1] then starting from 3rd element of vector fib we go on calculating **fib[i] = fib[i-1]+fib[i-2]** incrementing i till we reach i == n then we stop and return the vector fib in reverse.

Pseudocode:

```
function Fibonacci(index i):
    /*Create array of required length*/
    integer array fib[i+1]
    fib[0]=0
    fib[1]=1
    /*Loop over the array and calculate the
numbers at all positions*/
    for(i=2 to i+1)
        fib[i]=fib[i-1]+fib[i-2]
    return fib[i+1]
```

Following is the implementation in C++:

```
#include <iostream>
#include <vector>
using namespace std;

int main () {

    int n = 10;
    std::vector<int> V; // vector to store the
Fibonacci numbers.

    V.push_back(0); // fib(0) = 0
    V.push_back(1); // fib(1) = 1

    for(int i=2; i<=n; i++) {
        V.push_back(V[i-1] + V[i-2]); // fib(i) =
fib(i-1)+fib(i-2);
    }
    // reversing the vector to get required series
    int l = 0, r = V.size()-1;
    while(l<r){
        swap(V[l],V[r]);
```

```
        l++;
        r--;
    }
    // printing the Fibonacci series in reverse
order
    for(int element: V){
        std::cout<<element<<" ";
    }

    return 0;
}
```

Time Complexity:

T(N) = O(N)

Similar to recursive approach We never compute any Fibonacci number more than once also to compute any number we just perform two vector lookups of precomputed Fibonacci numbers hence our overall time complexity becomes O(N).

Longest Geometric Progression

In this chapter, we have explained how to solve the problem of Longest Geometric Progression efficiently using Dynamic Programming. It involves the use of Map data structure in implementation which is different from other standard problems.

Table of contents:

We can solve it via Naive Approach or via Dynamic Programming (where we have to use Map of Float Map<Float,Integer>).

Problem statement: Longest Geometric Progression

What is a Geometric Progression?

A sequence of elements is a Geometric Progression if it follows the following patterns:

a, a * r, a * r^2, ..., a * r^N, ...

where:

- a is the first element of the Geometric Progression
- a $*$ r^{i-1} is the ith element of the Geometric Progression

Let us first take example before solving the problem of Longest Geometric Progression:

A = {2, 4, 8, 10, 50, 250}

So, here we found 2 geometric progressions one of common ratio 2 and other with 5.

Yes, every two number will be in geometric sequence so we are discussing beyond that:

a_1: 2 4 8 , r=2

a_2: 2 10 50 250 , r=5

So, our answer should be 4 (size of a=2).

To better understand this problem, we need to observe some properties of geometric progression. Three numbers can be in geometric progression if and only if they hold property:

If a, b, c are in geometric progression:

$b^2 = a * c$

or we can say

b / a = c / b

Naive Approach

In Naive Approach, we will follow these steps:

- First sort the array. It will take O(N logN) time

- Traverse via a loop starting from first index and then nested one more loop for selecting next element for that progression.
- Now in inner most loop, we will check for all element which has same common ratio.

Time Complexity: **O(N³)**

Space Complexity: **O(1)** [depending on the sorting algorithm]

Dynamic Programming Approach

Algorithm

The structure of Dynamic Programming will be:

```
DP[i][j] = LGP with the first element
           being array[i] and ratio being j
```

LGP = Longest Geometric Progression

If there are two elements array[i] and array[j] with ratio R and there is no common ratio as compared to previous element pairs, then:

```
DP[i][R] = 1
```

Else if there is common ratio R among previous elements, then:

```
DP[i][r] = DP[j][r] + 1
```

Answer is the maximum value in the matrix DP[][].

To implement this technique efficiently with minimum space, you need to use a Map data structure.

Steps to find Longest Geometric Progression using Dynamic Programming:

- First sort all elements, so we can easily track number of elements which has same common ratio.
- Initialize an array of type (map<double,int>), length of array would be size of given set.
- Use two loops one for traversing our set and other for checking out which elements have same common ratio as previous ones. If we can find same common ratio then increment it with via 1, otherwise create a new entity for that map with common ratio and initialize it with two.

Step by step example

A = {5, 10, 20, 30}

So, size of array,

int n=A.size()

We will declare an array of map type which store the no of element which made a progression with a common ratio (r).

Now, how we think to solve this problem using dynamic programming, we have to maintain a list of map<float,integer> for every index of an array.

Let us trace the index of all array.

- Element at first index: 5

There is no element before this index so just continue

- Element at second index: 10

Before 10, we have an element at first index so common ratio r=10/5. With r=2, we update our map at second index list(2)(r) = 2.

- Element at third index: 20

Before this, we have two elements at first and second index. One with common ratio 2 and other we 4. With this, we update values as follows:

list(3)(2) = list(2)(2) + 1 = 3

list(3)(4) = 2

- Element at fourth index: 30

Here we got element with common ratio which has not come before.

list(4)(3/2) = 2

list(4)(3) = 2

list(4)(6) = 2

So, maximum value find at list(3)(2)=3

Answer = 3

Pseudocode

1: Declare map of float as a map value and Integer as a key Value Map<Float,Integer>dp

2: Now iterate from first index to last index and then put all values with common ratio in map and increment them

First check the size of given array. Let n be size of the array

if(n<=2) then simply n is our answer

otherwise, we have to declare an map of same size of array Map<Float,Integer>dp(n)

```
loop(i=0 to n)
{
  loop (j=0 to less than i)
  {
    float r=A[i]/A[j]
    Search r in dp[j]
      if r is present in dp[j] then
        dp[i][r] = dp[j][r] + 1   , because we found
one more value which has
        same common
```

152

```
             ratio.
           else
           Create an map with defaul value 2
           dp[i][r] =2 ,
           }
      }
```

Complexity

- Worst case time complexity: $\Theta(N^2)$
- Average case time complexity: $\Theta(N^2)$
- Best case time complexity: $\Theta(N^2)$
- Space complexity: $\Theta(N^2)$

Implementation:

```cpp
int findLargestSequence(int A[])
{
int n=sizeof(A)/sizeof(A[0]);
if(n<=2)
    return n;
sort(A,A+n); //first sort all the elements
map<float,int>dp[n]; // declare  a dp array of
size n.
int max=0;

for(int i=0;i<n;i++)
{
    for(int j=0;j<i;j++)
    {
        float r=A[i]/A[j];
        if(dp[j].find(r)!=dp[j].end());
        {
            dp[i].insert(make_pair(r,2));
```

```
            //sequence has at least two elements
with a ratio(r)
        }
        else
        {
            dp[i][r]=dp[j][r]+1;
            // if at the jth index we already have
a sequence with common ratio r
        }
        if(dp[i][r]>max)
            max=dp[i][r];
    }
}
return max;
}
```

Time & Space Complexity

- Time Complexity: $O(N^2)$
- Space Complexity: $O(N^2)$

Key Points:

1: We must have to map of float values because common ratio can be a float or decimal no both.

2: We have to sort the array.

Maximum Sum Rectangle in a Matrix

In this chapter, the problem we are going to discuss is - given a 2D array, we need to find the subarray with the maximum sum of its elements. As negative numbers can be present within the 2D array, this problem is challenging.

We solve this in two approaches:

- Brute force solution $O(N^5)$
- Dynamic Programming solution $O(N^3)$

Example:

1	2	-1	-4	-20
-8	-3	4	2	1
3	8	10	1	3
-4	-1	1	7	-6

From amongst all rectangles possible in the above matrix, the one marked across with the blue outline depicts the maximum sum rectangle (in this case, a square). All other configurations of rectangles have positive values of sum but the maximum sum for this example is 29.

This problem is an extension of Kadane algorithm for 2D matrices where Kadane's algorithm is for 1D array. Before going into the actual solution, we shall explore the brute force approach.

Brute Force solution O(N⁵)

Check every possible rectangle in the 2D array. With this approach, we need to select 2 row-indexes and 2 column-indexes and hence compute the sum of each possible rectangle. The maximum sum rectangle we obtain would provide us with the answer.

However, since the row and column indexes are variable, the problem requires four loops and with 2 inner loops to calculate the sum, the time-complexity of this approach is $O(N^6)$.

The time complexity of calculating the sum can be reduced from $O(N^2)$ to $O(N)$ using prefix sum array and hence, the time complexity can be brough down to $O(N^5)$.

Dynamic Programming solution O(N³)

This problem is mainly an extension of calculating the maximum sum contiguous subarray, which can easily be implemented using Kadane's algorithm.

Now we just need contiguous sets of rows that form a rectangle of maximum possible sum in the matrix. When values in the matrix are all positive the answer is pretty straight forward, the maximum sum rectangle is the matrix itself.

We use dynamic programming to reduce the brute force time complexity to O(N³).

The idea is to fix the left and right columns one by one and find the maximum sum contiguous rows for every left and right column pair.

We then find top and bottom row numbers for every fixed left and right column pair, which produces the maximum sum for us.

To find the top and bottom row numbers, calculate sum of elements in every row from left to right and store these sums in an array, say temp[]. Hence, temp[i] indicates the sum of elements from left to right in row 'i'.

If we apply Kadane's algorithm on temp[], and get the maximum sum subarray of temp, this maximum sum would be the maximum possible sum with left and right as boundary columns. To get the overall maximum sum, we compare this sum with the maximum sum obtained so far.

Kadane's Algorithm for 1D array:

```
1. initialize max_so_far = 0, max_ending_here = 0
2. loop for each element of the array
    a) max_ending_here += a[i]
```

```
  b) if(max_ending_here<0)
      max_ending_here = 0
    if(max_so_far<max_ending_here)
      max_so_far = max_ending_here
3. return max_so_far
```

In the above algorithm, two variables with the name
max_so_far and ma_ending_here are initially zero.

We keep on adding the elements of array to max_ending_here.
If the sum(max_ending_here) < 0, meaning negative elements
are not helpful in yielding maximum contiguous sum. If
max_so_far <max_ending_here, we store it.

On encountering negative elements that make
max_ending_here negative, max_ending_here is again zero and
we further calculate max_ending_here.If again the max_so_far
< max_ending_here,

We assign it again. Effectively, Kadane's algorithm calculates
sum within negative values occuring in the array and assigns the
maximum subarray sum to max_so_far.

Pseudocode for Kadane's Algorithm:

```
int kadane(vector<int>&arr)
{
    int n = arr.size()
    int max_so_far = 0, max_ending_here = 0

    for(int i=0; i<n; i++){
      max_ending_here = max(max_ending_here,
```

```
                    max_ending_here+arr[i])
    if(max_so_far<max_ending_here)
    max_so_far = max_ending_here
}

return max_so_far
}
```

-2	-3	4	-1	-2	1	5	-3

$$4 + (-1) + (-2) + 1 + 5 = 7$$

Explanation to the example above:

n = 8 //array size

max_so_far = 0, max_ending_here = 0

First iteration,

i=0, a[0] = -2

max_ending_here = max_ending_here + (-2)

max_ending_here = 0 as max_ending_here < 0

Second iteration,

i=1, a[1] = -3

max_ending_here = max_ending_here + (-3)

Set max_ending_here = 0 as max_ending_here < 0

Third iteration,

i=2, a[2] = 4

max_ending_here = max_ending_here + (4)

max_ending_here = 4

max_so_far is updated to 4 because max_ending_here greater

than max_so_far which was 0 till now

Fourth iteration,

i=3, a[3] = -1

max_ending_here = max_ending_here + (-1)

max_ending_here = 3 // no change here to

// make max_ending_here = 0

Fifth iteration,

i=4, a[4] = -2

max_ending_here = max_ending_here + (-2)

max_ending_here = 1

Sixth iteration,

i=5, a[5] = 1

max_ending_here = max_ending_here + (1)

max_ending_here = 2

Seventh iteration,

i=6, a[6] = 5

max_ending_here = max_ending_here + (5)

max_ending_here = 7

max_so_far is updated to 7 because max_ending_here is

greater than max_so_far

Eighth iteration,

i=7, a[7] = -3

max_ending_here = max_ending_here + (-3)

max_ending_here = 4

as (max_so_far = 7) > (max_ending_here = 4),

max_so_far = 7

return 7

Since number of iterations = array size,

time complexity of Kadane's Algorithm = O(n) // n, arr size

Pseudocode to extend Kadane's algorithm

Consider the following pseudocode where is find the rectangle with the maximum sum using Kadane's algorithm as a sub-routine:

```
int findMaxSum(int Matrix[][col])
{
    // Variables to store the final output
    int maxSum = INT_MIN;
    int finalLeft, finalRight, finalTop, finalBottom;
    //dimensions

    int left, right, i;   //left will iterate till col
    int temp[row], sum, start, finish;
    // temp[row] is auxiliary space

    // Set the left column
    for (left = 0; left < col; left++)
    {
        // Initialize all elements of temp as 0
        memset(temp, 0, sizeof(temp));

        // Set the right column for the left
        // column set by outer loop
        for (right = left; right < col; right++)
        {

            // Calculate sum between current left and right
for
            every row, i
    for (i = 0; i < row; i++)
      temp[i] += M[i][right];

            // Find the maximum sum subarray in temp[].
            // The kadane() function also sets values
            // of start and finish. So sum is sum of
            // rectangle between (start, left) and
            // (finish, right) which is the maximum sum
            // with boundary columns strictly as left
            // and right.
```

```
                    //call kadane() and store in sum
                    sum = kadane(temp, &start, &finish, row);

                    // Compare sum with maximum sum so far.
                    // If sum is more, then update maxSum and
                    // other output values to fix rectangle
dimensions
                    if (sum > maxSum)
                    {
                        maxSum = sum;
                        finalLeft = left;
                        finalRight = right;
                        finalTop = start;
                        finalBottom = finish;
                    }
                }
            }

    return maxSum;
}
```

Complete Implementation:

```
#include<bits/stdc++.h>
using namespace std;

int row
int col

/* Implementation of Kadane's algorithm for 1D array. This
function returns the maximum sum and stores start and end
indexes of the maximum sum subarray at addresses stored in
the start and finish respectively*/

int kadane(int* arr, int* start,
    int* finish, int n) //n is array size
```

```
{
    // initialize sum, maxSum and
    int sum = 0, maxSum = INT_MIN, i;   //INT_MIN is
minimum
                                        // integer value

    // for all negative values case
    *finish = -1;

    // local iterator if sum<0, start is local_start
    int local_start = 0;

    for (i = 0; i <n; i++)
    {
        sum += arr[i];
        if (sum < 0)
        {
            sum = 0;
            local_start = i + 1;
        }
        else if (sum > maxSum)
        {
            maxSum = sum;
            *start = local_start;
            *finish = i;
        }
    }

    // if atleast one non -ve number
    if (*finish != -1)
        return maxSum;

    // Special Case: When all numbers
    // in arr[] are negative
    maxSum = arr[0];
    *start = *finish = 0;   //maximum sum = 0

    // Find maximum element in array
    for (i = 1; i < n; i++)
    {
```

164

```
            if (arr[i] > maxSum)
            {
                maxSum = arr[i];
                *start = *finish = i;
            }
        }
        return maxSum;
}

//function to find maximum sum rectangle in Matrix[][]
int findMaxSum(int Matrix[][col])
{
        // Variables to store the final output
        int maxSum = INT_MIN;
        int finalLeft, finalRight, finalTop, finalBottom;
        //dimensions

        int left, right, i;   //left will iterate till col
        int temp[row], sum, start, finish;
        // temp[row] is auxiliary space

        // Set the left column
        for (left = 0; left < col; left++)
        {
            // Initialize all elements of temp as 0
            memset(temp, 0, sizeof(temp));

            // Set the right column for the left
            // column set by outer loop
            for (right = left; right < col; right++)
            {

                // Calculate sum between current left and right
for
                every row, i
        for (i = 0; i < row; i++)
            temp[i] += M[i][right];

                // Find the maximum sum subarray in temp[].
                // The kadane() function also sets values
```

```
                    // of start and finish. So sum is sum of
                    // rectangle between (start, left) and
                    // (finish, right) which is the maximum sum
                    // with boundary columns strictly as left
                    // and right.

                    //call kadane() and store in sum
                    sum = kadane(temp, &start, &finish, row);

                    // Compare sum with maximum sum so far.
                    // If sum is more, then update maxSum and
                    // other output values to fix rectangle
dimensions
                    if (sum > maxSum)
                    {
                        maxSum = sum;
                        finalLeft = left;
                        finalRight = right;
                        finalTop = start;
                        finalBottom = finish;
                    }
                }
            }
        }

    return maxSum;
}

// main
int main()
{
    int Matrix[ROW][COL] = {{1, 2, -1, -4, -20},
                            {-8, -3, 4, 2, 1},
                            {3, 8, 10, 1, 3},
                            {-4, -1, 1, 7, -6}};

    cout<<findMaxSum(Matrix);

    return 0;
}
```

Time Complexity Analysis

2 loops of iterators left and right run from 0 till col,

and the inner loop calls Kadane which is of linear complexity

and initialization of temp array is linear;

Time = $O(n) * O(n) * \{O(n) + O(n)\}$

Time = $O(N^3)$.

Thus, the time complexity of the above implementation is $O(N^3)$ which is better than the naive $O(N^5)$.

Question

Given a binary matrix, find the maximum size rectangle sub-matrix containing all 1's

Input:

```
0 0 1 0
1 1 1 0
0 1 1 1
1 0 0 1
```

Output:

```
1  1
1  1
```

Implement the above question using dynamic programming and analyze it's time and space complexity.

Concluding Note

As a next step, you may randomly pick a problem from this book, read the problem statement and dive into designing your own solution and implement it in a Programming Language of your choice.

Remember, we are here to help you. If you have any doubts in a problem, you can contact us (team@opengenus.org) anytime.

Dynamic Programming is a powerful Algorithmic technique which can help you tackle complex optimization and search problems easily.

Now on completing this book, you have conquered this core domain of Algorithm.

For more practice and contribute to Computing Community,
feel free to join our Internship Program:
internship.OPENGENUS.org